Current
CONTROVERSIES

States' Rights and the Role of the Federal Government

Other Books in the Current Controversies Series

Current
CONTROVERSIES

States' Rights and the Role of the Federal Government

Marcia Amidon Lusted, Book Editor

GREENHAVEN
PUBLISHING

Published in 2019 by Greenhaven Publishing, LLC
353 3rd Avenue, Suite 255, New York, NY 10010

Articles in Greenhaven Publishing anthologies are often edited for length to meet page
requirements. In addition, original titles of these works are changed to clearly present
the main thesis and to explicitly indicate the author's opinion. Every effort is made to
ensure that Greenhaven Publishing accurately reflects the original intent of the authors.
Every effort has been made to trace the owners of the copyrighted material.

Cover image: Mahesh Patil/Shutterstock.com

Library of Congress Cataloging-in-Publication Data

Names: Lusted, Marcia Amidon, editor.
Title: States' rights and the role of the federal government / Marcia Amidon
  Lusted, book editor.
Description: New York : Greenhaven Publishing, 2019. | Series: Current
  controversies | Includes bibliographical references and index. | Audience:
  Grade 9 to 12.
Identifiers: LCCN 2018003711| ISBN 9781534503137 (library bound) | ISBN
  9781534503144 (pbk.)
Subjects: LCSH: States' rights (American politics)—Juvenile literature. |
  Federal government—United States—Juvenile literature.
Classification: LCC JK311 .S735 2019 | DDC 320.473/049—dc23
LC record available at https://lccn.loc.gov/2018003711

Manufactured in the United States of America

Website: http://greenhavenpublishing.com

Contents

Chapter 2: Are States More Effective at Governance Than the Federal Government?

Yes: Efforts Must Be Made to Limit the Federal Government's Power and Restore Power to States

No: State Governments Are Less Effective Than the Federal Government

Chapter 3: Is the Federal Government Vital in Preventing States from Taking Unjust or Unwise Action?

Yes: The Federal Government Prevents States from Justifying and Passing Discriminatory or Otherwise Harmful Laws and Practices

No: States Require Discretion in How They Use Federal Funds and How to Best Address Their Citizens' Concerns

Chapter 4: Are States Better at Protecting Their Citizens' Interests Than the Federal Government?

Yes: States Have a Better Sense of Their Priorities, and the Federal Government Has Its Own Issues

No: The Federal Government, Through Its Funding and Programs, Is Better Able to Meet the Needs of States' Citizens

Foreword

Controversy is a word that has an undeniably unpleasant connotation. It carries a definite negative charge. Controversy can spoil family gatherings, spread a chill around classroom and campus discussion, inflame public discourse, open raw civic wounds, and lead to the ouster of public officials. We often feel that controversy is almost akin to bad manners, a rude and shocking eruption of that which must not be spoken or thought of in polite, tightly guarded society. To avoid controversy, to quell controversy, is often seen as a public good, a victory for etiquette, perhaps even a moral or ethical imperative.

Yet the studious, deliberate avoidance of controversy is also a whitewashing, a denial, a death threat to democracy. It is a false sterilizing and sanitizing and superficial ordering of the messy, ragged, chaotic, at times ugly processes by which a healthy democracy identifies and confronts challenges, engages in passionate debate about appropriate approaches and solutions, and arrives at something like a consensus and a broadly accepted and supported way forward. Controversy is the megaphone, the speaker's corner, the public square through which the citizenry finds and uses its voice. Controversy is the life's blood of our democracy and absolutely essential to the vibrant health of our society.

Our present age is certainly no stranger to controversy. We are consumed by fierce debates about technology, privacy, political correctness, poverty, violence, crime and policing, guns, immigration, civil and human rights, terrorism, militarism, environmental protection, and gender and racial equality. Loudly competing voices are raised every day, shouting opposing opinions, putting forth competing agendas, and summoning starkly different visions of a utopian or dystopian future. Often these voices attempt to shout the others down; there is precious little listening and considering among the cacophonous din. Yet listening and considering, too, are essential to the health of a democracy. If controversy is democracy's lusty lifeblood, respectful listening and careful thought are its higher faculties, its brain, its conscience.

Current Controversies does not shy away from or attempt to hush the loudly competing voices. It seeks to provide readers with as wide and representative as possible a range of articulate voices on any given controversy of the day, separates each one out to allow it to be heard clearly and fairly, and encourages careful listening to each of these well-crafted, thoughtfully expressed opinions, supplied by some of today's leading academics, thinkers, analysts, politicians, policy makers, economists, activists, change agents, and advocates. Only after listening to a wide range of opinions on an issue, evaluating the strengths and weaknesses of each argument, assessing how well the facts and available evidence mesh with the stated opinions and conclusions, and thoughtfully and critically examining one's own beliefs and conscience can the reader begin to arrive at his or her own conclusions and articulate his or her own stance on the spotlighted controversy.

This process is facilitated and supported in each Current Controversies volume by an introduction and chapter overviews that provide readers with the essential context they need to begin engaging with the spotlighted controversies, with the debates surrounding them, and with their own perhaps shifting or nascent opinions on them. Chapters are organized around several key questions that are answered with diverse opinions representing all points on the political spectrum. In its content, organization, and methodology, readers are encouraged to determine the authors' point of view and purpose, interrogate and analyze the various arguments and their rhetoric and structure, evaluate the arguments' strengths and weaknesses, test their claims against available facts and evidence, judge the validity of the reasoning, and bring into clearer, sharper focus the reader's own beliefs and conclusions and how they may differ from or align with those in the collection or those of classmates.

Research has shown that reading comprehension skills improve dramatically when students are provided with compelling, intriguing, and relevant "discussable" texts. The subject matter of these collections could not be more compelling, intriguing, or urgently relevant to today's students and the world they are poised to inherit. The anthologized articles also provide the basis for stimulating, lively, and passionate classroom debates. Students who are compelled to anticipate objections to their own argument and identify the flaws in those of an opponent read more carefully, think more critically, and steep themselves in relevant context, facts, and information more thoroughly. In short, using discussable text of the kind provided by every single volume in the Current Controversies series encourages close reading, facilitates reading comprehension, fosters research, strengthens critical thinking, and greatly enlivens and energizes classroom discussion and participation. The entire learning process is deepened, extended, and strengthened.

If we are to foster a knowledgeable, responsible, active, and engaged citizenry, we must provide readers with the intellectual, interpretive, and critical-thinking tools and experience necessary to make sense of the world around them and of the all-important debates and arguments that inform it. We must encourage them not to run away from or attempt to quell controversy but to embrace it in a responsible, conscientious, and thoughtful way, to sharpen and strengthen their own informed opinions by listening to and critically analyzing those of others. This series encourages respectful engagement with and analysis of current controversies and competing opinions and fosters a resulting increase in the strength and rigor of one's own opinions and stances. As such, it helps readers assume their rightful place in the public square and provides them with the skills necessary to uphold their awesome responsibility—guaranteeing the continued and future health of a vital, vibrant, and free democracy.

Introduction

The question of how power should be divided between the states and the federal government has been debated since the earliest days of the United States. Beginning with the Constitutional Convention of 1787, when a constitution for the new country was under discussion, there has been debate about how much power each level of government should hold. The Civil War was fought largely over this question, and it has been a central issue for many political parties and political campaigns for over two hundred years.

Part of the purpose of the Constitutional Convention was to replace the Articles of Confederation. The Articles were the United States' first written constitution and were ratified in 1781. The Articles were very different from the US Constitution, with the individual states remaining independent and sovereign and retaining ultimate power. Congress and the federal government served only as a last resort when there were disputes that the states could not settle independently. The federal government was also authorized to create treaties with foreign government, forge international alliances, mint money, and maintain an army. But the federal government could not create taxes or regulate commerce.

However, from the beginning of the American Revolution, it became clear that a stronger central government was needed if the colonies were going to defeat Great Britain. This was the beginning of a long debate about whether the United States should simply be a loose collection of states, self-governing without a strong central authority, or if such a large country required a more powerful central government. State leaders feared centralized authority, and it took many compromises to arrive at the present Constitution. The Constitution as we know it today preserves the sovereignty of the states in many respects, but there are some important provisions that limit their powers. Specific amendments to the Constitution convey the division of power, such as the Tenth Amendment, which maintains states' and citizens' powers:

Amendment X

The powers not delegated to the United States by the Constitution, nor prohibited by it to the States, are reserved to the States respectively, or to the people.

The Sixth Amendment, however, is called the Supremacy Clause because it delineates the supreme powers held by the federal government:

Article VI

This Constitution, and the Laws of the United States which shall be made in Pursuance thereof; and all Treaties made, or which shall be made, under the Authority of the United States, shall be the supreme Law of the Land; and the Judges in every State shall be bound thereby, any Thing in the Constitution or Laws of any State to the Contrary notwithstanding.

Article I, Section 10 makes it even more clear what individual states cannot do:

Article I, Section 10

No State shall enter into any Treaty, Alliance, or Confederation; grant Letters of Marque and Reprisal; coin Money; emit Bills of Credit; make any Thing but gold and silver Coin a Tender in Payment of Debts; pass any Bill of Attainder, ex post facto Law, or Law impairing the Obligation of Contracts, or grant any Title of Nobility.

No State shall, without the Consent of the Congress, lay any Imposts or Duties on Imports or Exports.[...]

No State shall, without the Consent of Congress, lay any Duty of Tonnage, keep Troops, or Ships of War in time of Peace, enter into any Agreement or Compact with another State, or with a foreign Power, or engage in War, unless actually invaded, or in such imminent Danger as will not admit of delay. [1]

The anti-Federalists, who opposed centralized authority for the United States, were against ratification of the Constitution, stating that these amendments and clauses gave too much power to the federal government and took it away from the states. The new Constitution was eventually ratified in 1787, but conflicts over the rights of the states versus the authority of the federal government continue to this day. Many people feel that the balance of power has now shifted too much to the federal government, with the growth of administrative agencies and federal programs that take away from states' powers. Today, many state governors have begun to defy the authority of the federal government, claiming it is overstepping its original boundaries and exceeding the constitutional limits of its power. Lawsuits over federal policies and laws—especially concerning issues like health care, the environment, same-sex marriage, and immigration—are one way that states attempt to regain power and freedom of choice for their citizens, particularly in an era when the federal government uses executive orders and legislation to overturn previous policies in a way that many states do not find agreeable.

The debate over the division of powers and whether states and their citizens should be able to resist federal policies and laws that are in direct opposition to what those states find to be important is a defining debate for the United States. Indeed, it is characteristic of any democratic republic—a country where some decisions, usually local, are made by direct democratic processes, while others, usually federal, are made by democratically elected representatives. *Current Controversies: States' Rights and the Role of the Federal Government* takes a look at the various arguments made for and against increasing the power of state governments.

Notes

1. "The Constitution of the United States." Constitution.us. Web. Accessed January 16, 2018. http://constitutionus.com/

Chapter 1

Should States Have Greater Control Than the Federal Government?

The Relationship Between State and Federal Governments

Annenberg Foundation

The Annenberg Foundation is a family foundation that supports environmental stewardship, social justice, and animal welfare.

Federalism is the division of powers between a central government and regional governments. Most developed nations experience ongoing struggles over the relative powers of their central and regional governments. The United States has a federal system of government where the states and national government exercise separate powers within their own spheres of authority. Other countries with federal systems include Canada and Germany. In contrast, national governments in unitary systems retain all sovereign power over state or regional governments. An example of a unitary system is France.

The framers of the U.S. Constitution sought to create a federal system that promotes strong national power in certain spheres, yet recognizes that the states are sovereign in other spheres. In "Federalist No. 46," James Madison asserted that the states and national government "are in fact but different agents and trustees of the people, constituted with different powers." Alexander Hamilton, writing in "Federalist No. 28," suggested that both levels of government would exercise authority to the citizens' benefit: "If their [the peoples'] rights are invaded by either, they can make use of the other as the instrument of redress." However, it soon became clear that Hamilton and Madison had different ideas about how the national government should work in practice. Hamilton, along with other "federalists" including Washington, Adams, and Marshall, sought to implement an expansive interpretation of national powers at the states' expense. Madison, along with other "states' rights" advocates including Thomas Jefferson, sought to bolster state powers.

The U.S. Constitution delegates specific enumerated powers to the national government (also known as delegated powers), while reserving other powers to the states (reserved powers). Article VI of the Constitution declares the laws of the national government deriving from the Constitution to be "the supreme law of the land" which the states must obey. The Tenth Amendment to the Constitution, a part of The Bill of Rights passed in 1791, attempts to limit national prerogatives over the states by declaring: "The powers not delegated to the United States by the Constitution, nor prohibited to it by the States, are reserved to the States respectively, or to the people."

While the Constitution carves out significant spheres of power for the states, it also contains several potential powers for the national government. These potential powers, also called implied powers, include Congress's power under Article I, Section 8, to make laws that are "necessary and proper" for carrying out its enumerated powers. The president's constitutional role as "commander in chief" has allowed presidents, including Lincoln, Franklin Roosevelt, and now George W. Bush, to claim emergency powers for the national government in times of national emergency. Finally, the Supreme Court's original delegated powers in Article III were significantly enhanced in the case of *Marbury v. Madison* (1802), where Chief Justice John Marshall first articulated the Court's power to exercise judicial review. Judicial review is the power to strike down as unconstitutional acts of the national legislature and executive, as well as state actions.

A review of American history shows that the lines that divide power between the national government and the states are blurry, and in practice the balance of powers between the two levels of government is constantly in flux. At the same time, certain periods of federalism can be identified, and are often associated with creative (although not always precise) metaphors:

- Dual federalism, also known as "layer cake federalism" involves clearly enumerated powers between the national and state governments, and sovereignty in equal spheres. This relationship predominated from the 1790s to 1930.
- Cooperative federalism, also known as "marble cake federalism," involved the national and state governments sharing functions and collaborating on major national priorities. This relationship predominated between 1930 and 1960.
- Creative federalism, also known as "picket fence federalism," predominated during the period of 1960 to 1980. This relationship was characterized by overloaded cooperation and crosscutting regulations.
- Finally, new federalism, sometimes referred to as "on your own federalism," is characterized by further devolution of power from national to state governments, deregulation, but also increased difficulty of states to fulfill their new mandates. This period began in 1981 and continues to the present.

There are other concepts of federalism that help describe the complicated relationships between the national and state governments. Judicial federalism involves the struggle between the national and state governments over the relative constitutional powers of each, and over key constitutional provisions including the Bill of Rights and the Fourteenth Amendment. With its power of judicial review, the Supreme Court is the arbiter of what the Constitution means on various questions, including federalism. Chief Justice John Marshall defended a national-supremacy view of the Constitution in the 1819 case of *McCulloch v. Maryland*. In that case the Supreme Court expanded the powers of Congress through a broad interpretation of its "necessary and proper" powers, and reaffirmed national supremacy by striking down Maryland's attempt to tax the Bank of the U.S.

Not all judicial decisions favor national power. In the 1997 case, *Printz v. United States*, for example, the court invalidated federal law that required local police to conduct background checks on all gun purchasers. The court ruled that the law violated the Tenth Amendment. Writing for the five-to-four majority, Justice Antonin Scalia declared: "The Federal government may neither issue directives requiring the states to address particular problems, nor command the states' officers, or those of their political subdivisions, to administer or enforce a Federal regulatory program.... Such commands are fundamentally incompatible with our constitutional system of dual sovereignty."

Fiscal federalism involves the offer of money from the national government to the states in the form of grants to promote national ends such as public welfare, environmental standards, and educational improvements. Until 1911, federal grants were used only to support agricultural research and education. With the passage of the Sixteenth Amendment in 1916, which legalized the federal income tax, the national government gained a significant source of revenue that it used to shape national policy in a variety of new policy areas.

Categorical grants, in which the national government provides money to the states for specific purposes, became a major policy tool of the national government during the New Deal era, and expanded rapidly during the 1960s' Great Society. But state and local officials began to criticize this method of national support because of the costly application and implementation procedures. They also complained that it was difficult to adapt the grants to local needs.

Beginning in the mid 1960s, block grants, which combined several categorical grants in broad policy areas into one general grant, became increasingly popular. States prefer block grants because they allow state officials to adapt the grants to their particular needs. Congress, however, is reluctant to use block grants because they loosen Congress's control over how the money is spent.

Revenue sharing was developed during the Nixon administration as a way to provide monies to states with no strings attached. Using statistical formulas to account for differences among states, the national government provided billions of dollars to the states until the program was abolished in 1986.

There are several pros and cons associated with U.S.-style federalism. Some advantages include a greater degree of local autonomy, more avenues for citizens to participate, and more checks and balances against concentrations of power. Some disadvantages include increased complexity of government that can produce duplication and inefficiency, and increased legal disputes between levels of government.

Constitutional Safeguards

Walter E. Williams

Walter Edward Williams is an American economist, commentator, and academic. He is a professor of economics at George Mason University, a syndicated columnist, and an author.

How often do we hear the claim that our nation is a democracy? Was a democratic form of government the vision of the Founders? As it turns out, the word democracy appears nowhere in the two most fundamental founding documents of our nation— the Declaration of Independence and the Constitution. Instead of a democracy, the Constitution's Article IV, Section 4, declares "The United States shall guarantee to every State in this Union a Republican Form of Government." Our pledge of allegiance to the flag says not to "the democracy for which it stands," but to "the republic for which it stands." Is the song that emerged during the War of 1861 "The Battle Hymn of the Democracy" or "The Battle Hymn of the Republic"?

So what is the difference between republican and democratic forms of government? John Adams captured the essence of the difference when he said, "You have rights antecedent to all earthly governments; rights that cannot be repealed or restrained by human laws; rights derived from the Great Legislator of the Universe." Nothing in our Constitution suggests that government is a grantor of rights. Instead, government is envisioned as a protector of rights.

In recognition that it is government that poses the gravest threat to our liberties, the framers used negative phrases in reference to Congress throughout the first ten amendments to the Constitution, such as shall not abridge, infringe, deny, disparage, and shall not be violated, nor be denied. In a republican form of government, there is rule of law. All citizens, including government

"Democracy or Republic?" by Walter E. Williams, Foundation for Economic Education, June 1, 2007. https://fee.org/articles/democracy-or-republic/. Licensed under CC BY 4.0 International.

officials, are accountable to the same laws. Government power is limited and decentralized through a system of checks and balances. Government intervenes in civil society to protect its citizens against force and fraud, but does not intervene in the cases of peaceable, voluntary exchange.

Contrast the framers' vision of a republic with that of a democracy. According to Webster's dictionary, a democracy is defined as "government by the people; especially: rule of the majority." In a democracy the majority rules either directly or through its elected representatives. As in a monarchy, the law is whatever the government determines it to be. Laws do not represent reason. They represent power. The restraint is upon the individual instead of government. Unlike the rights envisioned under a republican form of government, rights in a democracy are seen as privileges and permissions that are granted by government and can be rescinded by government.

There is considerable evidence that demonstrates the disdain held by our founders for a democracy. James Madison, in Federalist No. 10, said that in a pure democracy, "there is nothing to check the inducement to sacrifice the weaker party or the obnoxious individual." At the 1787 Constitutional Convention, Edmund Randolph said, "that in tracing these evils to their origin every man had found it in the turbulence and follies of democracy." John Adams said, "Remember, democracy never lasts long. It soon wastes, exhausts, and murders itself. There was never a democracy yet that did not commit suicide." Later on, Chief Justice John Marshall observed, "Between a balanced republic and a democracy, the difference is like that between order and chaos." In a word or two, the Founders knew that a democracy would lead to the same kind of tyranny the colonies suffered under King George III.

The framers gave us a Constitution that is replete with anti-majority-rule, undemocratic mechanisms. One that has come in for frequent criticism and calls for elimination is the Electoral College. In their wisdom, the framers gave us the Electoral College so that in presidential elections large, heavily populated states could not use their majority to run roughshod over small, sparsely populated states. Amending the Constitution requires a two-thirds vote of both houses of Congress, or two-thirds of state legislatures, to propose an amendment and three-fourths of state legislatures to ratify it. Part of the reason for having a bicameral Congress is that it places another obstacle to majority rule. Fifty-one senators can block the wishes of 435 representatives and 49 senators. The Constitution gives the president a veto to thwart the power of all 535 members of Congress. It takes two-thirds of both houses of Congress to override the president's veto.

There is even a simpler way to expose the tyranny of majority rule. Ask yourself how many of your day-to-day choices would you like to have settled through the democratic process of majority rule. Would you want the kind of car you own to be decided through a democratic process, or would you prefer purchasing any car you please? Would like your choice of where to live, what clothes to purchase, what foods you eat, or what entertainment you enjoy to be decided through a democratic process? I am sure that at the mere suggestion that these choices should be subject to a democratic vote, most of us would deem it a tyrannical attack on our liberties.

Most Americans see our liberties as protected by the Constitution's Bill of Rights, but that vision was not fully shared by its framers. In Federalist No. 84, Alexander Hamilton argued, " [B]ills of rights . . . are not only unnecessary in the proposed Constitution, but would even be dangerous. For why declare that things shall not be done [by Congress] which there is no power to do? Why, for instance, should it be said that the liberty of the press shall not be restrained, when no power is given [to Congress] by which restrictions may be imposed?" James Madison agreed: "This is one of the most plausible arguments I have ever heard urged against the admission of a bill of rights into this system . . . [because] by enumerating particular exceptions to the grant of power, it would disparage those rights which were not placed in that enumeration, and it might follow by implication, that those rights which were not singled out, were intended to be assigned into the hands of the general government, and were consequently insecure."

Madison thought this danger could be guarded against by the Ninth Amendment, which declares "The enumeration in the Constitution, of certain rights, shall not be construed to deny or disparage others retained by the people." Of course, the Ninth Amendment has little or no meaning in today's courts.

Transformed into a Democracy

Do today's Americans have contempt for the republican values laid out by our Founders, or is it simply a matter of our being unschooled about the differences between a republic and a democracy? It appears that most Americans, as well as their political leaders, believe that Congress should do anything it can muster a majority vote to do. Thus we have been transformed into a democracy. The most dangerous and insidious effect of majority rule is that it confers an aura of legitimacy, decency, and respectability on acts that would otherwise be deemed tyrannical. Liberty and democracy are not synonymous and could actually be opposites.

If we have become a democracy, I guarantee you that the Founders would be deeply disappointed by our betrayal of their vision. They intended, and laid out the ground rules for, a limited republican form of government that saw the protections of personal liberties as its primary function.

The Federal Government Makes It Difficult for States to Control Their Land Usage

Kevin Frazzini

Kevin Frazzini edits and writes stories on politics and policy for State Legislatures, *a magazine published 10 times a year by the National Conference of State Legislatures.*

The federal government has long had control issues when it comes to public lands in the West. It manages and pays for nearly everything that happens on more than 300 million acres, from recreation and wildlife conservation to mining, logging, grazing and oil and gas drilling.

This presents the states with a range of challenges as high and wide as the Western sky. Much of the land sits atop energy and mineral resources they'd love to develop. Federal lands are not subject to state or local taxes, of course, affecting revenue generation, and they sometimes wrap around state or private lands that do generate revenue, leading to conflict because of federal environmental regulations.

Furthermore, the Federal Land Policy Management Act stipulates that "public lands be retained in federal ownership." What's a state to do?

Since the federal act's passage in 1976, Western legislators have periodically chafed at what they claim are limits on their ability to manage the land inside their borders and develop their economies.

Land Locked

Those claims took on a renewed vigor in 2012 when the Utah Legislature passed the Transfer of Public Lands Act, sponsored by Representative Ken Ivory (R), a vocal proponent of conveying federal land to state control. Ivory founded the nonprofit American Lands Council, which advocates for "locally driven stewardship to improve public access, environmental health and economic productivity on public lands," according to its website.

Utah's law, which authorized suing the federal government if it didn't turn over more than 30 million acres to the state by the end of 2014, has resulted in a standstill: The feds haven't transferred title to any land, and so far the state hasn't filed suit, though it recently hired a firm to prepare a legal strategy.

The law "expressly takes off the table the national parks, congressionally designated wilderness and other national treasures," Ivory says. Utah lawmakers passed legislation last year supporting the 2012 bill, proving that measure wasn't a "land grab," as some critics have suggested, the American Lands Council says. Rather, it's "truly an effort to bring reasonable management and use practices to public lands in Utah and throughout the West."

For Ivory, it's a matter of fairness. "The federal government honored the promise to transfer title to the public lands to all states east of Colorado (and with Hawaii to our far west)," he said of his bill. "Yet, after 116 years, the federal government still controls more than 65 percent of Utah's lands and our abundant natural resources."

In recent years, at least 10 other states have considered legislation similar to Utah's. Most have passed measures that call for studies of the land-transfer issue, with attention to its economic feasibility and legality.

In Montana, for example, Senator Jennifer Fielder (R) backed a measure typical of others introduced throughout the West. It would have created a task force to study the ways Montana might benefit if the state, and not the U.S. government, managed the roughly 25 million acres of federal land within its boundaries.

Although the bill didn't pass, Fielder, like other advocates, says decisions on use and development are best made by the people closest to the issue—those living on or near the land in question.

"The goal is better management that improves access, environmental health and economic activity," she says. The federal government is so far removed from these lands there's "no accountability" for the way its decisions affect the people who live nearby, Fielder says.

The once-plentiful logging jobs in her rural district have become scarce largely because of federal land-management policies, she says.

Critics Cite Cost, Access

On the other side of what at times has been a partisan debate, land-transfer opponents—conservationists, hikers, hunters and anglers, among others—want to keep the feds involved in land-use decisions.

The biggest problem, they say, is the enormous cost of managing federal land. Paying for wildfire protection alone—it accounts for about half of the U.S. Forest Service's annual budget of $6.5 billion—would burden Western taxpayers, says the Center for Western Priorities, a conservation group.

States would be forced to raise taxes or sell off iconic national properties to developers or other private investors in order to pay for everything the federal government does now—from complicated tasks like enforcing environmental regulations and maintaining cultural and historic resources to simple ones like putting up road and trail signs.

Another problem is access. If states were to pay their bills by selling federal land gained from a transfer, the amount of land available to the public for hunting, fishing and recreation could be reduced to a patchwork.

Polls of Western voters have found attitudes toward land transfers vary, though a 2015 Colorado College State of the Rockies Project survey found a majority of voters in six Western states strongly believe public lands belong to all Americans, not just the residents of particular states.

Around the West

This year, the Arizona Legislature approved a measure to study the land-transfer issue, and Wyoming extended funding for a commission that's looking into state management. In Alaska, a bill to transfer federal lands to the state is pending.

In New Mexico, a bill that would have created a study commission died in part because of objections from conservationists and American Indian tribes. And in Colorado, a transfer-study bill died after conservationists and sportsmen rallied together at the state Capitol to "Keep public lands in public hands."

"Transferring control of public lands to the states is a budget-busting idea that is contrary to Colorado values of environmental protection and equal access to all on our open spaces and natural areas," the nonprofit group Conservation Colorado said.

Sportsmen echoed the group's concerns. "For hunters and anglers, our public lands are the backbone of our passions, and it's on public lands that we hunt and fish," Ty Churchwell, of Colorado Trout Unlimited, told the Durango Herald at the rally.

Complicated History

The deliberate approach Western states are taking on the land-transfer issue is no surprise. They've been here before.

The current debate echoes arguments made during the Sagebrush Rebellion of the late 1970s, when Nevada—the "Sagebrush State"—filed a lawsuit claiming the Bureau of Land Management territory inside its borders.

Starting in 1980, so-called sagebrush legislation was considered—if not passed into law—in almost every other Western legislature, Robert H. Nelson writes in a history of the movement. The rebellion's rhetoric suggested that federal land ownership was being forced on Western states by a domineering U.S. government.

The reality was that the West had found the rewards of federal ownership—the right to graze certain public lands at less than market rates, for example—to be worth the annoyances.

In the end, although the sagebrush rebels opened a debate in the West on land tenure, they did not persuade the region's opinion leaders or most of the key Western members of Congress to enact significant change.

Constitutional Hurdles

A further complication for the sagebrush rebels then and those who would renew the effort today is that the federal courts have not been sympathetic to the states' arguments, according to Martin Nie, director of the Bolle Center for People and Forests at the University of Montana.

"The courts have been consistent in their reading of the U.S. Constitution's Property Clause, which gives Congress proprietary and sovereign powers over its property and the power to delegate decisions regarding federal lands to executive agencies. The Supreme Court has repeatedly observed that this power over federal land is 'without limitations,'" Nie said in recent testimony to the Montana Legislature as part of a public land study.

There's also the problem that states officially and explicitly gave up their rights and title to federal lands within their borders as a condition of statehood.

Section four of Montana's law, for example, says the state "forever disclaim[s] all right and title to the unappropriated public lands lying within the boundaries thereof..."

Nie argues that beyond the legal issues there's a strong case for federal control of public lands, especially given big-picture concerns besides cost: the management of wide-ranging endangered species, the expansiveness of Western watersheds and the often long-lasting impacts of mineral and energy development. Despite the long odds, some state legislators argue all of these are tasks states can do, and do better than a federal agency.

A Way Forward

As long as legislators continue looking for greater control over land within their state boundaries and conservationists and outdoor enthusiasts remain wary of losing access to what they say belongs to all Americans, it's a near certainty that the land-transfer debate will continue.

Is there a middle way? Perhaps, if legislation Colorado passed recently is any indication. The new law offers local governments technical and financial support so they can address concerns about the management of federal lands without taking control of them. The text reads like a measured attempt to address anxieties on all sides:

"Early and consistent cooperative and collaborative involvement of local governments in federal land management decision-making processes can improve federal land management outcomes, reduce conflict and save state, local and federal resources."

The goal seems clear enough: Get people at the local and federal levels talking. Locals will feel they have more say in decisions that affect their jobs and lifestyle; the feds will be more responsive to local concerns when managing the vast resources in their care.

The bill passed with bipartisan support and was signed by the governor in May. "While the movement to transfer public lands to state control may have some merit, it's not likely to happen for a long time and not without a level of political support that doesn't yet exist," says Representative Bob Rankin (R), the bill's sponsor. "Meanwhile, there are many ways that our communities and the state can incrementally become better and stronger partners with federal land managers."

The law will both protect the environment and provide local officials with the money and expertise they need to develop their own plans for recreation, grazing and mineral development. "This is a practical response to what local governments are asking for," says Representative KC Becker (D), a co-sponsor.

Conservationists, as well, approved of the legislators' approach. In a statement, Conservation Colorado said, "House Bill 1225 represents the best of state and federal partners working together collaboratively as stewards of Colorado's incredible national public lands." The group congratulated legislators "for choosing to lead in a spirit of cooperation rather than dead-ended bluster and conflict."

Federal Land Management Can Work, but Working with States Is Necessary

Alexander Annett

Alexander Annett is a former environmental policy analyst for the Thomas A. Roe Institute for Economic Policy Studies at the Heritage Foundation.

Conserving America's land resources has been a federal concern since President Theodore Roosevelt made it a national priority more than 100 years ago. The objective was not just to conserve and protect the environment, but also to enhance the quality of life for Americans and improve the use of natural resources. Today, however, federal land management policy has strayed far from President Roosevelt's vision. Instead, Washington has implemented a command-and-control approach that wastes valuable financial resources and at times is environmentally harmful.

The federal government now owns one-third of the land in the United States. Four federal agencies—the Bureau of Land Management, Fish and Wildlife Service, Forest Service, and National Park Service—are tasked with managing most of this land with combined annual budgets of $8.1 billion for fiscal year (FY) 1999. But as recent reports by the federal government's own watchdogs point out, these agencies are not doing a good job. For example:

- The U.S. General Accounting Office (GAO) reported that the cost of eliminating the agencies' reported backlog of maintenance problems on public land exceeds $12 billion.
- The Inspector General of the U.S. Department of Agriculture found serious accounting and financial reporting deficiencies

"The Federal Government's Poor Management of America's Land Resources," by Alexander Annett, The Heritage Foundation, May 17, 1999. Reprinted by permission.

in the Forest Service, including "pervasive errors" in data supporting "land, buildings, equipment, accounts receivable, and accounts payable."

- A Congressional Research Service analyst found that a 1996 GAO study did not use a General Services Administration analysis of the amount of land each agency managed because of discrepancies between the GSA's numbers and those reported by the other four agencies.
- The Congressional Budget Office observed in April 1999 that President Clinton's Land Legacy Initiative would establish a $1.3 billion trust fund for new federal and state land acquisitions, which includes $450 million for federal land acquisition and $580 million for state and local government land acquisitions. This amounts to an increase of 125 percent over the federal funds available in the 1999 budget.
- The Conservation and Reinvestment Act of 1999 (H.R. 701) would direct about $900 million to the Land and Water Conservation Fund (LWCF)—$378 million for federal land acquisitions, $378 million for state land acquisitions, and $144 million for local governments' Urban Parks and Recreation Recovery programs. A companion bill (S. 25) has been introduced in the Senate. Unlike the Land Legacy Initiative, the congressional legislation would transform the LWCF into a "dedicated fund" that, by design, would allow federal agencies to bypass the scrutiny of the annual appropriations process and congressional oversight.

Such internal management problems, coupled with federal environmental regulations, undermine the efforts of federal land managers to care for public land under their oversight. Yet both President Bill Clinton and Congress have proposed establishing trust funds to purchase even more federal land which then would fall under these agencies' control.

As far back as 1818, the U.S. Supreme Court ruled in *U.S. v. Bevans* that a state's right to control property within its borders was an essential part of its sovereignty. Despite this precedent, however,

however, these new proposals would override both state sovereignty and private property rights.

As the Framers of the Constitution understood, people care most about the environment in which they live, and the level of government closest to the people is the most effective at implementing policies that promote conservation of land while respecting property rights. These current proposals, however, would enhance the federal government's appetite for—and its ability to own and manage—even more of the nation's lands, reducing even further the amount of private property owned by individual Americans. Thus, they run counter to America's constitutional legacy.

Today, the federal government cannot account fully for the quantity and condition of the land it owns. Congress's first step should be to initiate a thorough investigation of the federal government's current land holdings and land management activities. In addition, a new federal land management policy should be developed that is based on the core American principles of conservation, federalism, and property rights.

To that end, Congress should ensure that the federal government manages only public land possessing unique historic, recreational, or biological qualities. Privatizing land that should not be under government control would both ease the financial burden that inappropriate federal holdings inflict on taxpayers and the U.S. Treasury and encourage local interest and investment in conserving America's land resources.

Congress also should consider devolving to the states ownership of land that does not meet the criteria for federal ownership and is not suitable for privatization. State and local governments generally have managed public land efficiently and with greater responsiveness to local needs and interests. If their money had to pass first through Washington's land management bureaucracies, however, it is not certain that this would continue.

The implementation of policies that allow the federal government to own only land of truly national interest would accomplish two essential goals: It would enable federal land managers to focus their efforts and resources on protecting America's greatest national treasures, and it would ensure the long-term conservation of America's natural resources for future generations.

How Much Land Does Uncle Sam Own?

Although the goal of preserving land for posterity is noble, the true impact of current federal land management policy should not be lost behind a cloud of good intentions. In 1996, the General Accounting Office reported that the federal government owned a staggering 650 million acres, or one-third of the land in the United States. The Bureau of Land Management, the Forest Service, the Fish and Wildlife Service, and the National Park Service manage about 95 percent of this land (approximately 618 million acres, or about 7,500 acres per employee). As of September 1994, these agencies also had obtained rights-of-use to over 3 million acres on nonfederal land through leases, agreements, permits, and easements.

The Clinton Administration and several Members of Congress hope to enable the federal government to purchase even more land, which would then be placed under the management of these agencies. This effort by the federal government is not new:

- Between 1964 and 1993, the number of acres managed by the four federal agencies increased in 46 states and decreased only in Alaska, Idaho, New Mexico, and Utah.
- At the end of FY 1993, the four federal agencies managed over 50 percent of the land in five states and over 25 percent of the land in an additional seven states.
- Excluding two large land transfers in Alaska, the total amount of land managed by the four federal land management agencies between 1964 through 1993 increased by about 34 million acres.
- The four agencies acquired control of about 203,000 acres in FY 1994.

- In certain Western states and localities, the federal government owns the vast majority of land. For example, it owns more than 86 percent of the land in Nevada, 67.9 percent in Utah, 67 percent in Alaska, and 65.2 percent in Idaho.
- The Department of the Interior's budget for FY 2000 includes $295 million in land acquisition funds for 610,000 new acres.
- California is expected to lose over 445,000 acres to the federal government in FY 2000.

With few exceptions, the amount of land managed by the four federal land management agencies has increased, primarily through the expansion of existing national forests, wildlife refuges, and parks or through the creation of new ones. The proposals of the President and Congress would enable the federal government to spend up to $1.3 billion annually for federal and state land acquisitions, even though the federal land management agencies lack accountability and their track record can be characterized as poor.

How Well Are Federal Agencies Managing Public Land?

In an April 1999 report, the Congressional Budget Office proposed placing a ten-year moratorium on future appropriations for land acquisitions by land management agencies. Proponents of this option argue that these agencies should improve their stewardship of the land they already manage before taking on additional management responsibilities.

To facilitate their oversight of the preservation and protection of federal public lands, Members of Congress reasonably would expect the land management agencies to provide such information as the total amount of land managed, where it is located, the particular needs of each tract, and how these needs are reflected in agency performance goals, funding requests, programming, and staffing. In addition, under the Government Performance and Results Act, Congress expects agencies to match their performance goals with specific activities and to be held accountable for their results. The inability of federal land management agencies to provide Congress or the American public with an accurate accounting of the public lands under their control, in addition to their large backlog of maintenance problems, clearly indicates that these agencies are not performing as they should be.

[…]

A Better Approach to Land Stewardship

A recent poll found that approximately 70 percent of registered voters believe state and local governments would do a better job of environmental protection than the federal government can do. Yet, in almost all cases involving public land, federal agencies impose command-and-control regulations from Washington. The attempts by an inefficient federal bureaucracy to manage 650 million acres around the country have created a land management system that is both economically wasteful and environmentally harmful. Congress should work to decentralize ownership and management of public lands to the level of government, or to the people, affected most directly by the results of management practices.

In most cases, where the public land has no overriding national interest, Congress should consider an arrangement that allows privatization as well as state and local flexibility and experimentation to devise practical ways to manage and protect the land. State and private ownership of public land would tie the responsibility for land use policies to those who bear the impact of those policies. Differences in geography, economies, politics, and other factors would be addressed more appropriately. Until management of public land is made simpler and more efficient, America's land resources will continue to suffer.

Promoting Proper Management of Public Land

One way to address the problem of maintenance backlogs is to allow federal land managers to privatize various management functions and charge activity and land use fees to generate the revenue they need for operations and maintenance expenses. The incentives created by activity fee demonstration projects have shown good results.

For example, Congress authorized a demonstration program in 1996 that allowed the National Park Service, the Bureau of Land Management, the Fish and Wildlife Service, and the Forest Service to assess new or increased fees for recreational opportunities at up to 400 public sites. Fee collection systems were put in place at 312 sites. These agencies have reported that, because of this program, their combined recreational fee revenues doubled from about $93 million in FY 1996 to about $180 million in FY 1998. The Park Service collected 80 percent of the overall revenue, the Forest Service 15 percent, the Bureau of Land Management 3 percent, and the Fish and Wildlife Service about 2 percent.

The goal of such activity fee programs is to generate hundreds of millions of dollars to the agencies for visitor services, to address maintenance backlogs, and to promote resource conservation. Increases in the fees should cover the costs of recreation facility investments, operations, maintenance, and related services, especially where there is heavy public use.

Just as important as the success of the fee demonstration programs in raising operating funds is the GAO's conclusion that "visitation appears largely unaffected by the new and increased fees." Of the 206 sites in the demonstration program in FY 1997, visitation increased at 58 percent, decreased at 41 percent, and remained unchanged at 1 percent. By allowing the agencies to retain the fees collected, Congress created a powerful incentive for managers to focus on their needs, their programs, and their costs.

These types of revenue-generating demonstration programs should not be limited to recreational opportunities. Programs should be implemented to allow agencies to obtain fair market value for other uses of the resources on the land, such as timber production and grazing. Such programs would create an incentive for agencies to raise revenue to cover their maintenance needs and help to relieve the burden on the U.S. Treasury to fulfill those needs.

The 650 million acres controlled by the federal government encompass a wealth of forest, grazing land, minerals, wildlife, and recreational amenities with enormous potential for generating revenues for the public good. However, according to a study published by the Political Economy Research Center (PERC), the Forest Service and the Bureau of Land Management lost an average of $290 million in timber production, $66 million in grazing, and $355 million in recreation activities from 1994 through 1996. The reason for this loss of revenue, according to this study, was cost inefficiencies. Because these agencies are funded by Congress and do not have to rely on their own earnings to operate, they have little incentive to cut costs or maximize revenue. Yet the Administration and many Members of Congress appear willing to entrust these agencies with more land.

States as Models of Stewardship

In contrast to federal land agencies, state land management agencies generally have been more cost-efficient managers. The states earn profits from allowing mining, logging, grazing, and recreation activities on public land. Between 1994 and 1996, ten Western states earned a combined average of $5.56 per dollar spent managing state trust lands, compared with $0.30 earned per dollar spent by the Forest Service and $0.94 earned per dollar spent by the Bureau of Land Management. Not only do the federal land agencies earn far less than state agencies do, but they also outspend the states on a per-acre basis. In fact, on average, the Forest Service spends more than five times what the states spend, and the Bureau of Land Management spends nearly twice what the states do.

What Federal Management Costs the States. Currently, the United States government owns 50 percent or more of the land in 180 counties. Local communities and states are unable to collect taxes on this property or to sell or lease the acreage to generate revenue. Such property taxes could be used to fund school systems, police and fire departments, libraries, and other local and state government functions. As a result, federal land holdings impose costly economic burdens on communities and large financial commitments on the American taxpayer.

To compensate local governments for lost revenues that result from an inability to assess property taxes on federally owned land, Congress passed the Payment in Lieu of Taxes (PILT) law. Under the current formula, Congress promised over $260 million in PILT payments per year. On average, Congress promised the counties $0.43 per acre under the PILT formula. However, funding for PILT has fallen each of the past six years. In FY 1998, funding fell to an all-time low; Congress funded 45.6 percent of the payments it promised under the PILT formula.

Privatization and devolution of public land would lessen this economic impact on local communities and allow the federal land management agencies to focus on the needs of lands that properly belong under federal control.

[...]

State and Federal Health Care Reform in Conflict

Richard Cauchi

Richard Cauchi is Health Program Director at the National Conference of State Legislatures (NCSL) Denver office, where he directs projects and research on health finance and costs, health insurance, and pharmaceuticals.

In response to the federal health reform law, the Patient Protection and Affordable Care Act (PPACA or just ACA)*, and separate state reform initiatives, some members of at least 48 state legislatures proposed legislation to limit, alter or oppose selected state or federal actions. The results on the state level, as of July 1, 2016, vary widely, as detailed below and in separate NCSL reports on Health exchanges and on Medicaid expansion.

2015–2016 Court Updates

- On June 25, 2015 the U.S. Supreme Court voted 6-3 to uphold health insurance subsidies for people who purchased their insurance through a federal health insurance exchange. The ruling in *King v. Burwell* means that 6 million to 7 million people will continue to receive insurance subsidies.
- In June 2012, the U.S. Supreme Court upheld most provisions of the Patient Protection and Affordable Care Act, but rejected the portion of the law that would have penalized states that did not comply with the expanded eligibility requirements for Medicaid, making expansion optional and a state decision.
- 2016 cases: Additional cases continue in 2016-17, especially on paying insurers for the cost-sharing assistance.

"State Laws and Actions Challenging Certain Health Reforms," by Richard Cauchi, National Conference of State Legislatures, March 25, 2017. © National Conference of State Legislatures. Reprinted by permission.

Measures Enacted and Passed by States

Between 2010 and 2016, at least 22 state legislatures had enacted laws and measures related to challenging or opting out of broad health reforms related to mandatory provisions of the Patient Protection and Affordable Care Act (ACA).

Missouri: 2010 law provides that it is against Missouri public policy to implement or operate a health insurance exchange in Missouri.

2015-16 Sessions: A much smaller number of bills were considered - Earlier opposition enacted laws were expanded or amended in Arizona, Arkansas, South Carolina, and Tennessee. See NCSL's Innovations database for listings.

2014 Sessions: As of Dec. 30 at least 181 bills and resolutions in 38 states include opposition to, or proposed legislative alternatives to substantive provisions in the ACA. For 2014,15 such bills have been signed into law, in ten states.

2013 Sessions: As of December 2013, there were 81 bills in 32 states, territories or D.C. that relate to challenges, opposition or alternatives to health reform.

Summary of Enacted Provisions

The 22 state laws and measures related to challenging or opting out of broad health reform including the Patient Protection and Affordable Care Act (PPACA) vary, using at least three general approaches. Additional states have enacted measures considered non-conforming with the stated goals of the ACA, such as non-expansion of Medicaid, non-participation in the operation of the health exchange or marketplace, blocking individual health benefits such as contraception, or restrictions on navigators. These are detailed and tallied in other reports:

- Legislative approval required. Nine states, Arizona, Arkansas, Georgia, Missouri, Montana, New Hampshire, North Carolina, Utah and Wyoming, have passed restrictions on further compliance with PPACA unless approved by the legislature. The most recent actions were during 2015 in Arizona and Arkansas.

- The individual and employer coverage mandate has been a primary focal point for state opposition. Eighteen states currently have statutory or state constitutional language providing that state government will not implement or enforce mandates requiring the purchase of insurance by individuals or payments by employers. Because the U.S. Supreme Court upheld the individual coverage mandate, which does not require a state role, the federal law fully applies and any contradictory state laws will have no current effect on PPACA provisions. These state laws do aim at barring state agencies and employees from enforcing fines and penalties, as of 2014. These actions are distinct from the 26 states that were parties to the federal court challenge ruled on by the Supreme Court on June 28, 2012.

- Interstate Health Compacts. Separately, nine states have recently enacted laws intended to create Interstate Health Compacts— these take a first step toward allowing a group of states to join together to establish broad health care programs that operate outside of the PPACA or other federal law. However, these compacts do not block PPACA implementation, and are not yet binding; they will require congressional approval because they seek to substitute state control where federal law and regulations exist. These states (including Alabama, Georgia, Indiana, Kansas (2014) Missouri, Oklahoma, South Carolina, Utah and Texas) aim to obtain "primary responsibility for regulating health care goods and services" within their boundaries. Utah repealed most of their compact statute in 2014.

- State Nullification. While 23 states have considered bills seeking to nullify the legal validity of the ACA, none of the bills have become law in their original form. One state, North Dakota, has enacted a law using portions of model state nullification language. S. 2309 establishes by statute that, "The legislative assembly declares that the federal laws known as (PPACA) likely are not authorized by the United States Constitution and may violate its true meaning and intent as given by the founders and ratifiers." The original bill as filed provided that the ACA is "considered to be null in this state" and making it a criminal offense for any federal official to implement the ACA; however these two provisions were deleted and omitted from the signed law.

- Restricting use of Navigators. More than a dozen states have enacted laws regulating and/or restricting the functions of navigators and others who assist consumers in selecting health insurance in exchanges or Marketplaces. These measures are detailed in another NCSL report on Exchanges.

The legal language opposing reforms varies from state to state and includes statutes and constitutional amendments, as well as binding and non-binding state resolutions.

Nine state legislatures adopted some type of non-binding resolution or memorial to the federal government.

The challenge by state legislation approach garnered state legislative interest during 2009-2012 in significant part due to the American Legislative Exchange Council's (ALEC) model "Freedom of Choice in Health Care Act," which the organization described as "How Your State Can Block Single-Payer and Protect Patients' Rights." The ALEC-endorsed language mirrors Arizona Proposition 101, which was narrowly defeated in 2008 but passed on their November 2010 ballot.

2011–2015 Highlights of Completed Legislative Actions

Signed Laws and Binding Resolutions for Ballot Questions

Alabama - HB 60, passed House and Senate; enacted without governor›s signature, June 9, 2011. Opposes elements of federal health reform, providing by constitutional amendment that residents may provide for their own health care, and that "a law or rule shall not compel any person, employer, or health care provider to participate in any health care system." This amendment required voter approval or disapproval on the November 6, 2012 ballot. "Amendment 6" Passed with 59.0% Yes votes.

Alabama - HB 109, enacted, became law as Act No. 2013-420, May 20, 2013. Establishes the interstate "Health Care Compact" in the state of Alabama, allowing states that join the compact to propose state health policies that could replace federal provisions, citing, "Each member state, within its state, may suspend by legislation the operation of all federal laws, rules, regulations and orders regarding health care that are inconsistent with the laws and regulations adopted by the member state pursuant to this compact." The laws also seeks to use appropriated federal funds, redirected to state-specified programs. The interstate compact plan requires prior approval by the U.S. Congress before it becomes a recognized as interstate compact.

Arizona - H 2643, enacted, signed into law by the governor, April 10, 2015. Prohibits the "funding or implementation of a state-based health care exchange or marketplace." Also prohibits the state and political subdivisions "from using any personnel or financial resources to enforce, administer or cooperate with the Affordable Care Act."

Arkansas - HB 1053, signed into law by the governor as Act No. 276, March 13, 2014. Restricts ACA-related activities by providing that the State Insurance Department shall not allocate, budget, expend, or utilize any appropriation authorized by the General Assembly for the purpose of advertisement, promotion, or other activities designed to promote or encourage enrollment in the Arkansas Health Insurance Marketplace or the Health Care Independence Program, including unsolicited communications mailed to potential recipients; television, radio, or online commercials; billboard or mobile billboard advertising; advertisements printed in newspapers, magazines, or other print media; and Internet websites and electronic media. Also would prohibit responding to an inquiry regarding the coverage for which a potential recipient might be eligible, including without limitation providing educational materials or information regarding any coverage for which the individual might qualify. Also see S 111.

Arkansas - SB 111, signed into law by the governor as Act No. 257, March 7, 2014. Provides that the Dept. of Human Services, Div. of Medical Services shall not allocate, budget, expend, or utilize any appropriation authorized by the General Assembly for the purpose of advertisement, promotion, or other activities designed to promote or encourage enrollment in the Arkansas Health Insurance Marketplace or the Health Care Independence Program, including without limitation, unsolicited communications mailed to potential recipients; television, radio, or online commercials. Also see H 1053.

Arkansas - S 343, signed by the governor, March 12, 2015. Prohibits the establishment through existing state law of a state-based health insurance exchange in the state under the ACA. Referencing the *King v. Burwell* case before the U.S. Supreme Court, it requires a "future act of the General Assembly" for any action related to the previously authorized "Arkansas Health Insurance Marketplace" or its board.

Florida - H 1193, passed House and Senate; signed by the governor as Chapter No. 2011-126, June 2, 2011. By state statute, prohibits a person from being compelled to purchase health insurance except under specified conditions including dangerous occupation, voluntary enrollment in public benefits or contracts between private parties.

Florida - S 2, passed Senate and House; sent to the secretary of state, 5/4/2011. Joint resolution proposes a State Constitutional amendment to prohibit laws or rules from compelling any person, employer, or health care provider to participate in any health care system, permit any person or employer to purchase lawful health care services directly from health care provider, or permit health care provider to accept direct payment from person or employer for lawful health care services. This amendment required voter approval or disapproval on the November 6, 2012 ballot. "Amendment 1" Failed, with 48.5% Yes votes.

Georgia - H 461, passed House and Senate; signed by the governor as Act 10, April 20, 2011. Adopts the interstate Health Care Compact; provides for member state control over personal health care decisions; vests regulatory authority to the states; provides that member states resolve by the adoption into law provisions of the Health Care Compact to define health care as including an individual or group plan that provides or pays the cost of health care, services, or supplies; provides for the right to federal monies.

Georgia - H 943, H 990 both passed House and Senate as amended (from H 707); signed by the governor, April 15, 2014. Prohibits any agency or state action to expand Medicaid or accept any federal grant money to establish a state-run health exchange. Also ends the Univ. of Georgia Health Navigator Program. Titled "Georgia Health Freedom Law;" goes into effect July 1.

Indiana - S 461, passed Senate and House; signed by the governor as Public Law No. 160-2011, May 12, 2011. Provides by statute that "a resident of Indiana may not be required to purchase coverage under a health plan. A resident may delegate to the resident's employer the resident's authority to purchase or decline to purchase coverage under a health plan." Also authorizes consumer protections, rate review and rescissions compatible with the ACA. Note: Other provisions restricting agencies from implementing ACA provisions were deleted from the final enacted bill.

Indiana - H 1269 of 2012; signed by the governor as Chapter 150 of 2012 on March 19, 2012. Authorizes the state to join the "Health Care Compact," requiring member states of the compact to take action to secure the consent of Congress for the compact; asserting that member states of the compact have the primary responsibility to regulate health care in their respective States. Also seeks to establish that "Each member state, for the member state's jurisdiction, may, to the extent allowed under the Constitution of the United States and the constitution of the member state, suspend by legislation federal laws, regulations, and orders concerning health care that are inconsistent with the laws and regulations adopted by the member state under the compact." Also creates the Interstate Advisory Health Care Commission and would assert the rights of member states to certain federal health money.

Kansas - H 2182, passed House and Senate; signed by the governor, May 25, 2011. Opposes specific provisions of federal health reform, providing (in Sec. 7) by state statute that "The government shall not interfere with a resident's right to purchase or refuse to purchase health insurance." Also provides that residents, employers and health providers "shall not be required to pay penalties or fines" for direct payment without using health insurance; the "government shall not enact a law" that "would impose a form of punishment for exercising these rights." Effective date is July 1, 2011.

Kansas - H 2553 of 2014, passed House and Senate; signed by the governor, April 22, 2014. Accepts and adopts membership in the Health Care Compact; provides that each member state, within its state, may suspend by legislation the operation of all federal laws, rules, and regulations, and orders regarding health care that are inconsistent with the laws and regulations adopted by the member state pursuant to the compact.

Kentucky - H 265, passed House and Senate, signed by the governor, April 11, 2012. 2012-14 Appropriations act section 10, authorizes the state to "to explore the feasibility of an Interstate Reciprocal Health Benefit Plan Compact (IRHBPC) with contiguous states" to allow Kentucky and residents of contiguous states to purchase health benefit plan coverage among the states participating with the compact. The purposes of this compact are, through means of joint and cooperative action among the compacting states to promote and protect the interest of consumers purchasing health benefit plan coverage. (Note: this law is not a challenge to the provisions of PPACA; it is included as an alternative approach, for comparative information purposes.)

Missouri - H 45, passed House and Senate; signed by the governor, 7/8/2011. Provides that "any federal mandate implemented by the state shall be subject to statutory authorization of the general assembly." Creates a new $20,000 employer tax deduction for each new full-time job created with an annual salary of at least the average annual county wage if the small business also offers new employee health insurance and pays at least 50% of the health insurance premiums of all full-time employees who opt into the offered plan. Any new proposed rule must "Certify that the rule does not have an adverse impact on, or must exempt small businesses with fewer than fifty full- or part-time employees."

Missouri - H 423, passed House and Senate; became law without governor's signature, 7/14/2011. Establishes the interstate Health Care Compact, which would pledge member states to act jointly to oppose certain elements within health reform.

Missouri - S 464, passed Senate and House, sent to Secretary of State, 5/31/2012; governor's signature not required. Would amend state law chapter 376, a new section relating to the authority for creating and operating health insurance exchanges in Missouri. Would prohibit the establishment and operation of health insurance exchanges in Missouri unless the exchange is created by a legislative act, an initiative petition, or referendum, requiring voter approval. S 464, as Proposition E, was on the statewide ballot November 6, 2012 for a binding vote. "Proposition E" Passed with 61.8% Yes votes.

Montana - S 125, passed Senate and House; governor›s amendments rejected; signed by the governor as Chapter 402, May 13, 2011. Opposes elements of federal health reform, providing that by state law state agencies "may not implement or enforce in any way the provisions" or any federal regulation or policy implementing federal health reform "that relates to the requirement for individuals to purchase health insurance and maintain minimum essential health insurance coverage." Bars public employers or state employees from implementing or enforcing participation in the individual mandate to purchase health insurance.

Montana - S 418, passed House and Senate; enacted as Chapter

Montana - S 418, passed House and Senate; enacted as Chapter 310 and sent to the Secretary of State, May 4, 2011. Would prohibit, by state statute, the federal and state government from mandating the purchase of health insurance coverage; would prohibit imposing penalties related to health insurance decisions. The act will be submitted by referendum to voters for approval or disapproval in the November 2012 state election.

New Hampshire - S 148, passed Senate and House; became law as Chapter 266 without governor›s signature, 7/14/2011. Provides by insurance statute that a resident of New Hampshire shall not be required to obtain, to maintain, or be assessed a fee or fine for failure to obtain health insurance coverage. Effective date July 1, 2011.

New Hampshire - H 601, Passed House and Senate; became law as Chapter 264 without governor›s signature, 7/14/2011. By statute, requires that before establishing standards for enforcing the provisions of the federal Affordable Care Act, the insurance commissioner shall obtain approval from a newly created N.H. legislative Health Insurance Reform Oversight Committee. The provision applies to enforcing the immediate "consumer protections and market reforms." Effective date July 1, 2011.

New Hampshire - S 1297, passed Senate and House, signed by the governor as Chapter No. 2012-231, June 18, 2012. Prohibits the state from establishing a state based health insurance exchange. Also provides that in the event a federally-facilitated exchange is established for New Hampshire, the insurance commissioner retains authority with respect to insurance products sold in New Hampshire "on the federally-facilitated exchange to the maximum extent possible by law." Also required the state attorney general to join the lawsuit challenging the Patient Protection and Affordable Care Act and require federal grant moneys received by the state for implementation of the PPACA to be returned to the federal government. Effective date June 18, 2012.

North Carolina - S 4 was enacted as Act No. 2013-5, March 6, 2013. By state law, it specifies the state›s intent not to operate a state-run or "partnership" health benefit exchange, providing that future Medicaid eligibility determinations would be made by the state rather than the federally facilitated exchange, also rejects the Affordable Care Act›s optional Medicaid expansion. It does permit use of federal grants for premium rate review.

North Dakota - H 1165 was enacted and signed by the governor, April 4, 2011; providing by state law that a resident is not required to have a policy of individual health coverage, and would not be "liable for any penalty, assessment, fee, or fine." Applies regardless of whether the resident has or is eligible for health insurance coverage under a policy, through an employer or under a plan administered by the state or federal government. Continues an exception if health coverage is required by a court or by the state Department of Human Services through a court or administrative proceeding.

North Dakota - S 2309 was enacted and signed by the governor, April 27, 2011. [Full text] Using parts of model language invoking "nullification," establishes by statute that, "The legislative assembly declares that the federal laws known as (PPACA) likely are not authorized by the United States Constitution and may violate its true meaning and intent as given by the founders and ratifiers." ... no provision "may interfere with an individual's choice of a medical or insurance provider except as otherwise provided by the laws of this state."

Ohio - Issue #3, a citizen-initiated constitutional amendment was approved by voters on the November 8, 2011 ballot. It seeks to preserve their "freedom to choose their health care and health care coverage." It passed 66 percent Yes to 34 percent No. Similar pending Ohio legislation was not enacted in 2011-2012 (as of 8/10/12).

Oklahoma - S 722 was enacted and signed by the governor, May 18, 2011. Adopts the interstate Health Care Compact; provides for member state control over personal health care decisions; vests regulatory authority to the states; provides that member states resolve by the adoption into law provisions of the Health Care Compact to define health care as including an individual or group plan that provides or pays the cost of health care, services, or supplies.

South Carolina - H 3700 State budget for fiscal year 2011-12 was enacted and signed by the governor, August 2, 2011. It includes Section 89.126, that provides that "If federal law permits, the State of South Carolina opts out of "certain provisions in the Affordable Care Act, including the individual mandate or minimum coverage requirement, the employer contribution requirement, and insurance expansions including coverage for adult dependents up to age 26. (It does not reference enforcement by state officials or agencies)

South Carolina - S 836, passed Senate and House, signed by the governor as Act 221, 6/21/2012. Enacts state participation in the Interstate Healthcare Compact; providing that state compact members must take action to obtain congressional consent to the compact; providing that the legislature is vested with the responsibility to regulate healthcare delivered in their state; provides for healthcare funding; also establishes the S.C. interstate advisory Health Care Commission.

South Carolina- the state budget for FY 2016 and FY 2017 contained language prohibiting or restricting the state role with health exchanges or other state implementation unless the legislature gave prior approval to such provisions.

Tennessee - S 79 was enacted and signed by the governor as Chapter 9, March 18, 2011. A statute declaring it state public policy that every person within the state "shall be free to choose or to decline to choose any mode of securing health care services without penalty or threat of penalty;" it requires that no state or local public official, employee, or agent "shall act to impose, collect, enforce, or effectuate any penalty in this state."

Tennessee - H 937, enacted and signed by the governor, 4/14/2014. Prohibits, by statute, the state, the TennCare or Medicaid program or its residents from participating in any state option for Medicaid eligibility expansion authorized under the federal PPACA.

Tennessee - SJR 91 was adopted and signed –Signed resolution 4/30/2015. Non-binding resolution; requests lawsuit against any fines.

Texas - SB 7, passed Senate, passed House, 96y-48n, 6/27/2011; signed by the governor, July 19, 2011. State market reform act; includes an interstate health care compact, allowing Texas to partner with other states to ask the federal government for control — both fiscal and governmental — over Medicare, Medicaid and commercial coverage; also directs state officials to seek a waiver from Washington to operate Medicaid with a federal block grant.

Utah - H 175 and S 208 of 2012 - Passed House and Senate; signed by the governor, 3/19/2012. Provides by statute that the state join an interstate Health Care Compact, including a pledge to take joint and separate action to secure congressional approval "in order to return the authority to regulate health care to the member states." Would seek to authorize that "Each member state, within its state, may suspend by legislation the operation of all federal laws, rules, regulations, and orders regarding health care that are inconsistent with the laws and regulations adopted by the member state pursuant to this compact."

Utah - H 131 of 2013 - signed by the governor as Chapter 101, 3/26/13. Renames the Constitutional Defense Council and creates the Commission on Federalism; provides for the repeal of the State Health Compact by July 1, 2014, and subjects these provisions to a 10-point sunset review prior to repeal.

Virginia - SB 283 passed Senate and House and became law as Chapter 106 of 2010 on March 10, 2010 becoming the first such statute in the nation. Amends state law by adding a section, "Health insurance coverage not required. No resident of this Commonwealth, regardless of whether he has or is eligible for health insurance coverage under any policy or program provided by or through his employer, or a plan sponsored by the Commonwealth or the federal government, shall be required to obtain or maintain a policy of individual insurance coverage. No provision of this title shall render a resident of this Commonwealth liable for any penalty, assessment, fee, or fine as a result of his failure to procure or obtain health insurance coverage." It does not apply to Medicaid and CHIP coverage.

Wyoming - SJR 2, approved by both House and Senate by a 2/3rds vote; governor's signature not required. A constitutional amendment, stating that residents have the right to make their own health care decisions, while "any person may pay, and a health care provider may accept, direct payment for health care without imposition of penalties or fines for doing so." Also provides that the state "shall act to preserve these rights from undue governmental infringement." Approved by voters on the November 6, 2012 ballot by majority vote.

Wyoming - S 58 of 2012 - Enacted by Senate and House; signed by the governor as Chapter 61, 3/9/2011. Amends the duties of the Wyoming Health Insurance Exchange Steering Committee to require a study report with 3 options including 1) an exchange based on Wyoming data without influence from the health care reform acts, 2) using selected parts of required federal features and 3) an exchange in complete compliance with the Act. The statute limits the state's authority to operate a federally required health insurance exchange, restating that "No state agency or any person representing the state of Wyoming shall, prior to April 1, 2013, commit the state" to operating an exchange.

[...]

* PPACA also has been commonly termed "Obamacare," a name referenced within some state filed legislation.

CHAPTER 2

Are States More Effective at Governance Than the Federal Government?

How State Governments Operate

Vote Smart

Vote Smart's mission is to provide free, factual, unbiased information on candidates and elected officials to all Americans.

T he following is a general background on how state government works. Please note that each state operates according to its own constitution.

Powers Reserved for the Federal Government

The U.S. government is federal in form. The states and national government share powers, which are wholly derived from the Constitution.

From the Constitution, the national government derives

- express powers
- implied powers
- inherent powers

Article I, Section 10 of the Constitution of the United States puts limits on the powers of the states. States cannot form alliances with foreign governments, declare war, coin money, or impose duties on imports or exports.

Powers Reserved to the States

The Tenth Amendment declares, "The powers not delegated to the United States by the Constitution, nor prohibited by it to the states, are reserved to the states respectively, or to the people." In other words, states have all powers not granted to the federal government by the Constitution.

"Government 101: State Governments," Vote Smart. Reprinted by permission.

These powers have taken many different forms. States must take responsibility for areas such as:

- ownership of property
- education of inhabitants
- implementation of welfare and other benefits programs and distribution of aid
- protecting people from local threats
- maintaining a justice system
- setting up local governments such as counties and municipalities
- maintaining state highways and setting up the means of administrating local roads
- regulation of industry
- raising funds to support their activities

In many areas, states have a large role but also share administrative responsibility with local and federal governments. Highways, for example, are divided amongst the three different levels. Most states classify roads into primary, secondary, and local levels. This system determines whether the state, county, or local governments, respectively, must pay for and maintain roads. Many states have departments of transportation, which oversee and administer intrastate transportation. U.S. highways and the interstate system are administered by the national government through the U.S. Department of Transportation.

Mandates

States must also administer *mandates* set by the federal government. Generally these mandates contain rules which the states wouldn't normally carry out. For example, the federal government may require states to reduce air pollution, provide services for the handicapped, or require that public transportation must meet certain safety standards. The federal government is prohibited by law from setting unfunded mandates. In other words, the federal government must provide funding for programs it mandates.

Grants

Grants are an important tool used by the federal government to provide program funding to state and local governments. According to the Office of Management and Budget, federal outlays for grants to state and local governments increased from $91 billion in fiscal year 1980 (about $224 billion in 2013 constant dollars) to about $546 billion in fiscal year 2013. (See figure). Block grants give the states access to large sums of money with few specific limitations. The state must only meet the federal goals and standards. The national government can give the states either *formula grants* or *project grants* (most commonly issued).

Mandates can also pass from the state to local levels. For example, the state can set certain education standards that the local school districts must abide by. Or, states could set rules calling for specific administration of local landfills.

State Constitutions

The Basics

Each state has its own constitution which it uses as the basis for laws. All state governments are modeled after the federal government and consist of three branches: executive, legislative, and judicial. The U.S. Constitution mandates that all states uphold a "republican form" of government, although the three-branch structure is not required.

Therefore, in basic structure state constitutions much resemble the U.S. Constitution. They contain a preamble, a bill of rights, articles that describe separation of powers between the executive, legislative and judicial branches, and a framework for setting up local governments.

Length and Specificity

State constitutions also tend to be significantly more lengthy than the U.S. Constitution. State constitutions can contain as many as 174,000 words (Alabama), and have as many as 513 amendments attached (also Alabama). Much of this length is devoted to issues or areas of interest that are outdated. Oklahoma's constitution, for example, contains provisions that describe the correct temperature to test kerosene and oil. California has sections that describe everything that may be deemed tax-exempt, including specific organizations and fruit and nut trees under four years of age.

Amendment
All state constitutions provide for a means of amendment. The process is usually initiated when the legislature proposes the amendment by a majority or *supermajority* vote, after which the people approve the amendment through a majority vote. Amendments can also be proposed by a constitutional convention or, in some states, through an initiative petition.

The Legislature
All states have a bicameral, or two-house legislature, except Nebraska, which has a unicameral, or single, house. Legislative salaries range from nothing (Kentucky and Montana) to $57,500 (New York) per year. In states where there is no official salary, legislators are often paid on a per diem basis (i.e. Rhode Island Legislators earn $5 per day).

The Upper House
- called the Senate.
- membership can range from 21 (Delaware) to 67 (Minnesota).
- terms usually last four years.

The Lower House
- called the House of Representatives, General Assembly, or House of Delegates (Virginia),
- membership can range from 40 (Alaska and Nevada) to 400 (New Hampshire).
- terms usually last two years.

Leadership

Like the national legislature, each house in a state legislature has a presiding officer. The Lieutenant Governor presides over the Senate, but the majority leader assumes most of the leadership roles. The house elects a Speaker who serves as its leader. Leaders of each house are responsible for recognizing speakers in debate, referring bills to committee, and presiding over deliberations.

States grant legislatures a variety of functions:

- Enact laws
- Represent the needs of their constituents
- Share budget-making responsibilities with Governor
- Confirm nominations of state officials
- House begins impeachment proceedings, Senate conducts the trial if there is an impeachment.
- Casework
- Oversight - review of the executive branch. (e.g., *sunset legislation*)

Citizen Legislation

Legislators don't wield the only legislative power in state government. In many states, the people can perform legislative functions directly. The ways by which these methods can be implemented vary, but they usually require a certain number of signatures on a petition. After that, the issue is put on the ballot for a general vote.

- Initiative - A way citizens can bypass the legislature and pass laws or amend the state constitution through a direct vote.
- Referendum - A way citizens can approve of statutes or constitutional changes proposed by the legislature through a direct vote.
- Recall - A way citizens can remove elected officials from office. It is allowed in 14 states and is hardly ever used.

Governor

The Governor is a state's chief executive. A governor can serve either a two or four year term. Thirty-seven states have term limits on the governor.

Roles:

- Appointments
- The Governor is chiefly responsible for making appointments to state agencies and offices. These powers include:
- The ability to appoint for specific posts in the executive branch.
- The ability to appoint to fill a vacancy caused by the death or resignation of an elected official
- Chief of State
- Chief Executive - draws up budget, also has clemency and military powers
- Veto Power
- Like the U.S. President, a governor has the right to veto bills passed by the legislature.
- Vetoes can be overridden by a two-thirds or three-fourths majority in the legislature.
- In many states, the governor has the power of a line-item veto.
- In some states, the governor has the power of an amendatory or conditional veto.

Other Elected Positions Within the Executive Branch

The president and vice-president are the only elected executive positions within the federal government. State governments, however, often have other positions executive elected separately from the governor. Some examples include:

- Lieutenant Governor: Succeeds the governor in office and presides over the senate.
- Secretary of State - Takes care of public records and documents, also may have many other responsibilities.
- Attorney General - Responsible for representing the state in all court cases.

- Auditor - Makes sure that public money has been spent legally.
- Treasurer - Invests and pays out state funds.
- Superintendent of Public Instruction - Heads state department of education.

Revenue

A government's revenue system is the entire means by which a government acquires funding. States rely on a broad range of revenue sources to fund government. On average, states generate more than one-third of their revenues from personal income taxes and another one-third from general sales taxes. The remaining revenues are split between excise taxes (on gasoline, cigarettes and alcohol); corporate income and franchise taxes; and taxes on business licenses, utilities, insurance premiums, severance, property and several other sources. That being said, the general character of a state or state and local revenue system is more important than the nature of any single one of its components.

The relative importance of the major revenue sources for state and local governments changed since 1971. Property taxes declined in importance, and their share was picked up mostly by state individual income taxes, charges and miscellaneous revenues. Since state revenue systems have developed gradually and tax policy is used to address multiple objectives, state revenue systems are likely to include inconsistencies.

- Insurance Trust Revenue relates to the money that the state takes in for administering programs such as retirement, unemployment compensation, and other social insurance systems.
- Services and Fees include items such as tolls, liquor sales, lottery ticket sales, income from college tuition, hospital charges and utility fees.
- State Taxes come in many different forms: Most states have a sales tax. The sales tax is assessed on most consumer goods in the state and ranges from 4% to 7%. Most states also have a state income tax, similar to the

one used by the federal government. People can pay up to 16% of taxable income in state income taxes. Most states have a progressive sales tax. About 37% of state tax revenue is obtained through the personal income tax. Corporate income tax is also assessed on corporate income, a sum that accounts for 7% of state tax revenue. States levy taxes on motor fuels such as gasoline, diesel, and gasohol. Most of the funds go towards financing roads and transportation within the state. Sin taxes apply to alcoholic beverages and tobacco products. These taxes are named as such because they were originally intended to decrease consumption of these "undesirable" goods. Most states also have inheritance taxes, where a person pays a percentage of what he or she inherits from a deceased person.

- Lotteries: In 2011, 43 states, the District of Columbia, Puerto Rico, and the U.S. Virgin Islands have adopted some sort of gambling, most in the form of instant-winner or "drawing" lotteries. About 1 percent of state revenue comes from gambling. Lotteries can be very profitable for the state. Profits from lotteries have been used towards funding education, economic development, and environmental programs. Net income from state lotteries was over $17.75 billion in 2010.
- Debt: Like the Federal government, state governments also have debts. In 2012, total state government debt had reached $757 billion. Debts range from about $114 million in Wyoming to over $120 billion in California.

Education

One of the largest issue areas left to the discretion of the states is education. The United States' public education system is administered mostly on the state and local levels. Elementary and Secondary schools receive funding from all the different levels of government: about 8% from the Federal Government, 50% from the State government, and 42% from local governments. State and local governments put more money toward education than any other cost. There are approximately 15,000 school districts around the country, each governed by its own school board. The people of the district vote the members of the school board into office. Generally about 15-30% of the local electorate participate in a typical school board election. Some roles of a school board:

- Administer general district policy
- Make sure the district is in tune with local interests
- Hire or fire the superintendent

The Superintendent is the head administrator within a district. His or her responsibilities include:

- Drafting the budget
- Overseeing the principals of schools within the district
- General administration within the district
- Communication with the chief state school official (CSSO).

The chief state school official is appointed by the governor and, along with other state education positions, has many responsibilities:

- distribute state funds
- establish teacher certification requirements
- define length of the school day
- defines nutritional content of school lunches
- mandate certain curricula for schools and set the school calendar

State Government Vocabulary

amendatory or conditional veto - the power to send a bill back to the legislature with suggested changes.

casework - taking care of constituents' problems; "errand-running" for particular individuals.

express powers - powers which are directly specified in the Constitution.

federal - a system in which the states and national government share responsibilities. When people talk about the federal government, they generally mean the national government, although the term often refers to the division of powers between the state and national governments.

formula grants - grants given to anyone who meets certain guidelines (grants such as those for school lunches, airports or highways).

implied powers - powers which are not explicitly stated in the constitution, but which are implied through the "necessary and proper" clause in Article I, Section 8.

inherent powers - powers which the national government naturally has to represent the country in relations with other countries.

line-item veto - the power of a governor to veto particular lines (items) in budget appropriations bills.

mandate - a requirement set by the national government to force states to perform a particular action.

presiding officer - one person who oversees the activities of a legislative house. A presiding officer can have either a major or minor leadership role in his or her house.

project grants - grants given to those who make special requests for aid.

progressive tax - a tax where people with higher incomes pay a higher percentage of taxable income in state taxes.

sunset legislation - legislation that has a specific expiration or renewal date. Sunset legislation can be used in several situations.

It can be used to persuade legislators who do not strongly support a particular measure. When the legislation lasts only a set length of time, the "on the fence" legislators are more likely to vote for it because of its "temporary" nature.

Some issues change rapidly (e.g., technology-related issues), and therefore legislation pertaining to these issues must be updated periodically.

supermajority - a vote which takes a quantity greater than the majority, usually 2/3 or 3/4, to pass.

term limit - a limit on the number of consecutive terms an elected official can serve.

unfunded mandate - when the federal government sets regulations for the states to follow and does not provide the states with funds to carry them out.

Federal Powers Should Not Extend Beyond Those Enumerated in the Constitution

National Governors Association

The National Governors Association (NGA) is the bipartisan organization of the nation's governors.

The relationship and authority of states and the federal government are governed by the U.S. Constitution. The federal government is delegated certain enumerated powers while all other powers not otherwise prohibited by the Constitution are reserved to the states. America has thrived as a nation of laws with a strong national and international identity anchored by the diversity and innovation of representative self government in the states. It is vital that the National Governors Association works to preserve and promote a balanced relationship between the states, territories and the Commonwealth of Puerto Rico (herein referred to as "States") and the federal government.

Principles for State-Federal Relations

Governors believe that federal action should be limited to those duties and powers delegated to the federal government under the Constitution. We favor the preservation of state sovereignty when legislating or regulating activity in the states. To ensure the proper balance between state and federal action and to promote a strong and cooperative state-federal relationship, governors encourage federal officials to adhere to the following guidelines when developing laws and regulations.

"Principles for State-Federal Relations," National Governors Association. Reprinted by permission.

Exercise Federal Forbearance

Governors recommend that:

- Federal action should be limited to situations in which constitutional authority for action is clear and certain.
- Federal action should be limited to problems that are truly national in scope.
- Federal action should be sensitive to each state's ability to bring a unique blend of resources and approaches to common problems.
- Unless the national interest is at risk, federal action should not preempt additional state action.

Avoid Federal Preemption of State Laws and Policies

Governors recognize the need for federal intervention should states fail to act collectively on issues of legitimate concern. Preemption of state laws, however, should be the exception rather than the rule. This is especially true in areas of primary state responsibility, including education, insurance regulation, criminal justice, preservation of the dual banking system, preservation of state securities regulation, and the management of state personnel programs.

- Congress should not interfere with state revenue systems. The independent ability of states to develop their own revenue systems is a basic tenet of self government and our federalist system. The federal government should not enact any legislation or adopt any regulation that would preempt, either directly or indirectly, sources of state revenues, state tax bases, or state taxation methods.
- State standards should be preserved. In cases where Congress determines that federal preemption of state laws is in the national interest, federal legislation should:
- accommodate state actions taken before its enactment;
- permit states that have developed stricter standards to continue to enforce them; and

- permit states that have developed substantially similar standards to continue to adhere to them without change.
- The judicial branch should respect state authority. Avoiding federal preemption of state laws and policies also extends to the judicial branch. Governors encourage the federal courts to restore the Tenth Amendment as a substantive limit on federal intrusion into areas of state and local concern, and place meaningful limits on the federal government's scope of authority under the Commerce Clause. In addition, court-ordered remedies should respect state authority by limiting the time and scope of injunctive relief and by extending it no further than is necessary to restore the exercise of constitutional rights. The federal courts also should exercise forbearance in policy areas that have traditionally been state responsibilities and avoid substituting their judgments for those of state legislatures and Governors absent violations of the U.S. Constitution.

Avoid Imposing Unfunded Federal Mandates

Congress and the Administration should avoid the imposition of unfunded federal mandates on states. Federal action increasingly has relied on states to carry out policy initiatives without providing necessary funding to pay for these programs. State governments cannot function as full partners in our federal system if the federal government requires states to devote their limited resources toward complying with unfunded federal mandates.

Designing Federal-State Programs

To provide maximum flexibility and opportunity for innovation, as well as foster administrative efficiency and cross-program coordination, federal-state programs should be designed to meet the following principles:

- States should be actively involved in a cooperative effort to develop policy and administrative procedures.

- The federal government should respect the authority of states to determine the allocation of administrative and financial responsibilities within states in accordance with state constitutions and statutes. Federal legislation should not encroach on this authority.
- Legislation should authorize and appropriate sufficient funds to meet identified program objectives.
- Federal assistance funds, including funds that will be passed through to local governments, should flow through states according to state laws and procedures.
- States should be given flexibility to transfer a limited amount of funds from one grant program to another, or to administer related grants in a coordinated manner.
- Federal funds should provide maximum state flexibility without specific set-asides.
- States should be given broad flexibility in establishing federally mandated advisory groups, including the ability to combine advisory groups for related programs.
- Governors should be given the authority to require coordination among state executive branch agencies, or between levels or units of government, as a condition of the allocation or pass-through of funds.
- Federal government monitoring should be outcome-oriented.
- Federal reporting requirements should be minimized.
- The federal government should not dictate state or local government organization.

Conclusion

Governors recognize the unique nature of the federal system and the critical importance of developing a close working relationship with our federal partner. We also recognize and support a continued federal role in protecting the basic rights of all our citizens and in addressing issues beyond the capacity of individual states. At the same time, the federal government must recognize that there are problems that can be best addressed at the state and local levels.

Governors are committed to a vibrant and strong partnership with Congress and the Administration to maintain and promote a balanced federal system. Governors believe that a strong, cooperative relationship between the states and federal government is vital to best serve the interests of all citizens.

The Federal Government Must Be Held Accountable

Democracy Web

Democracy Web is a project of the Albert Shanker Institute. It is an online resource for the study of democracy.

> *"A popular Government without popular information or the means of acquiring it, is but a Prologue to a Farce or a Tragedy or perhaps both. Knowledge will forever govern ignorance, and a people who mean to be their own Governors must arm themselves with the power knowledge gives."*
>
> -James Madison, Letter to W. T. Barry, August 4, 1822

> *"[T]he concentration of power and the subjection of individuals will increase amongst democratic nations . . . in the same proportion as their ignorance."*
>
> -Alexis de Tocqueville, Democracy in America, Vol. 2, 1840

In a democracy, the principle of accountability holds that government officials — whether elected or appointed by those who have been elected — are responsible to the citizenry for their decisions and actions. In order that officials may be held accountable, the principle of transparency requires that the decisions and actions of those in government are open to public scrutiny and the public has a right to access government information. Both concepts are central to the very idea of democratic governance. Without accountability and transparency, democracy is impossible. In their absence, voters are necessarily ignorant in their electoral choices; elections and the notion of the will of the people lose their meaning and government has the potential to become arbitrary and self-serving.

The People's Right to Know

Elections are the primary means for citizens to hold their country's officials accountable for their actions in office, especially when they have behaved illegally, corruptly, or ineptly in carrying out the government's work. For elections — and the people's will — to be meaningful, basic rights must be protected and affirmed, as through the Bill of Rights in the United States. James Madison, the author of the Bill of Rights, believed that the very basis for government's responsiveness was the assurance that citizens would have sufficient knowledge to direct it. If citizens are to govern their own affairs, either directly or through representative government, then they must be able to have access to the information needed in order to make informed choices about how best to determine their affairs. If citizens and their representatives are not well informed, they can neither act in their own self-interest, broadly speaking, nor can they have any serious choice in elections, much less offer themselves as candidates.

A free media is the essential guarantor of the public's access to information. The media must have broad protection against infringements of its rights and responsibilities under the Constitution, and must have the freedom to be able to search out information when the public interest is concerned and be able to publish information relevant to the public's interests.

The people must also have the right to know about government proceedings and have the right to gain access to government information. The US Constitution established that the proceedings of the Congress must be published regularly (and the US President must report regularly on the "state of the nation"). In general, however, the right to access government information has been entrenched in the law only with the passage of the Freedom of Information Act in 1966. In signing the precedent-setting law, US president Lyndon Johnson stated:

> [T]his legislation springs from one of our most essential principles: a democracy works best when the people have all the information that the security of the nation permits. No one

should be able to pull the curtains of secrecy around decisions which can be revealed without injury to the public interest.

Absent these instruments for accountability and transparency, government is likely to succumb to corruption and the general abuse of power. This has occurred throughout history when no controls have been placed on governmental actions and leaders have sought merely to retain their positions of power and privilege.

Separation of Powers

Accountability also involves the separation of powers, which is the principle that no branch of government may dominate another, and that each branch has the power to check fundamental abuses by other branches. For example, Congress's authority, granted by the US Constitution, gives it the power to hold the other branches accountable for breaches of the public's trust through impeachment and expulsion. US federal courts, especially the Supreme Court, have the authority to judge the constitutionality of congressional laws and the executive branch's actions to faithfully carry out those laws. Parliamentary systems do not have separation of powers in the same way, since the executive branch is appointed by the legislature. In such systems, standards of accountability are established through tradition, laws, and oversight by opposition political parties, an independent judiciary, public commissions, and a free press. Ultimately, however, accountability is found in parliament's power to withdraw its majority support for a government in power through votes of no confidence.

A federal system of government provides additional separation of powers by delegating power to states or regions to have control over the public's affairs that are not determined at the national level. In the US, the 10th Amendment of the Bill of Rights reserves to the individual States (or the people themselves) all public matters that are not delegated to the United States — the whole of the country embodied in the structure of the national government — or prohibited to the States (such as the making of money). A similar principle is subsidiarity, found in the laws of the European

Union (EU), which establishes that decisions should be made at the lowest level of government possible so that citizens are closest to the decision-making structures, thereby allowing for greater accountability. Principles of federalism or subsidiarity often conflict in significant ways with the setting of national priorities or the protecting of individual rights. In US history and contemporary politics, such built-in tensions have been constant. Yet, the basic principle remains central to the idea of accountability — it is difficult for national governments to be accountable to all local needs.

The Advantages of Democracy over Dictatorship

Governments that are truly accountable can more effectively prevent corruption, which involves the use of positions of power or privilege for personal, corporate, or group enrichment. Corruption, of course, is possible in all systems of government and democracies are not immune to it. Still, democracies have several advantages in dealing with corruption. One is that elected representatives in a democracy have a direct relationship with the country's citizens. Indeed, the various laws, constitutional provisions and internal regulations found in democracies reflect the idea that those who work for the government, whether appointed, elected or hired, owe a high level of accountability to the people, namely the taxpayers who pay their salaries.

By contrast, dictatorships have no such protections or safeguards. Leaders in a dictatorship do not have the same incentives as leaders in a democracy to avoid violating the law and abusing power to their own advantage. Government positions are owed to the dictator (or those serving a dictator) and indeed often dictators encourage officials to abuse their power through corruption in order to gain their loyalty.

The correlation of dictatorship and corruption is certainly much higher than in democracies. The 2015 Corruption Perceptions Index compiled by Transparency International (TI), a global organization committed to fighting corruption, demonstrates the connection. On one end of the scale, out of the top 50 countries ranked least corrupt in TI's "perception surveys" (out of a total of 168 surveyed), 40 are categorized as "free" in Freedom House's Survey of Freedom in the World 2015, four as "partly free," and six as "not free." At the opposite end of the spectrum, of the 50 most corrupt countries in the TI index, 30 are in the "not free" category in Freedom House's survey and 20 are "partly free," with most of these bordering on the "not free" category.

Accountability and transparency tends to help create better policies and stop the abuse of power. The more the public knows about the government's actions, the better judgements it can make about public policy. This is especially so in the case of abuse of power. In the United States, the media, the courts, and the legislature all played key roles in uncovering a conspiracy by President Richard Nixon and his staff to use illegal means to undermine his opponents and tip Nixon's 1972 re-election bid in his favor. In democracies, leaders have resigned or been removed from office when it was made public that they used their power and privilege to financially benefit themselves and their friends, repaid election gifts with legislative favors, or engaged in disreputable personal behavior. Even if leaders are not forced from office, the uncovering and investigating of malfeasance or inappropriate actions can sometimes bring about positive changes in leaders' governance or behavior. Still, there is significant concern within democracies about the corrupting and corrosive impact of private interests in the funding of elections and how this affects public policy and laws. This is especially so in the United States.

Representative and Private Organizations in Democracies and Dictatorships

In democracies, standards of accountability and transparency affect not only government, but also businesses, groups, and organizations that operate under public laws. When one speaks of corruption in this context, it usually involves the payment of bribes to powerful government officials in exchange for special treatment or favors regarding lucrative business transactions or other economic activities. But corruption can exist within corporations, trade unions, humanitarian organizations, civic groups, schools, hospitals, political parties, and other voluntary organizations. Democracies generally adopt laws that require all such public, corporate, civic, or representative organizations to conduct their operations in a manner designed to ensure that the interests of the members, stakeholders, and the general public are properly served and that these institutions do not violate the public's trust.

In addition, international groups often attempt to establish universal standards designed to prevent corruption, such as the UN Convention Against Corruption. The OECD and Council of Europe have adopted even more specific measures that are used in regional initiatives, such as in Eastern Europe, while the United States has backed the Open Government Partnership, which is committed to providing data about the way public money is spent.

In dictatorships, while private organizations may exist, many become instruments of the state and are used to control the broader society, enrich the ruler, or benefit his or her closest associates. In communist states, trade unions are controlled by the official structures of the Communist Party. While membership is obligatory, the unions generally do not operate on behalf of the workers, their members, but to serve to centralize control over the workforce (see, for example, Country Studies of China, Cuba, and Vietnam). In some countries, the purpose of privately-run, state-owned companies is to enrich government officials while strengthening the powers of the state (such as Gazprom in Russia). In dictatorships, all of these entities generally fuel a high level of corruption.

States Are Not Offering Adequate Financial Support for Education

Michael Mitchell, Michael Leachman, and Kathleen Masterson

Michael Mitchell, Michael Leachman, and Kathleen Masterson hold administrative positions at the Center on Budget and Policy Priorities (CBPP), which informs college students about how the increase in tuition costs has been handled by the states.

Years of cuts in state funding for public colleges and universities have driven up tuition and harmed students' educational experiences by forcing faculty reductions, fewer course offerings, and campus closings. These choices have made college less affordable and less accessible for students who need degrees to succeed in today's economy.

Though some states have begun to restore some of the deep cuts in financial support for public two- and four-year colleges since the recession hit, their support remains far below previous levels. In total, after adjusting for inflation, funding for public two- and four-year colleges is nearly $10 billion below what it was just prior to the recession.

As states have slashed higher education funding, the price of attending public colleges has risen significantly faster than the growth in median income. For the average student, increases in federal student aid and the availability of tax credits have not kept up, jeopardizing the ability of many to afford the college education that is key to their long-term financial success.

States that renew their commitment to a high-quality, affordable system of public higher education by increasing the revenue these schools receive will help build a stronger middle

"Funding Down, Tuition Up," by Michael Mitchell, Michael Leachman and Kathleen Masterson, Center on Budget and Policy Priorities, August 15, 2016. http://www.cbpp.org. Reprinted by permission.

class and develop the entrepreneurs and skilled workers that are needed in the new century.

Of the states that have finalized their higher education budgets for the current school year, after adjusting for inflation:

- Forty-six states — all except Montana, North Dakota, Wisconsin, and Wyoming — are spending less per student in the 2015-16 school year than they did before the recession.
- States cut funding deeply after the recession hit. The average state is spending $1,598, or 18 percent, less per student than before the recession.
- Per-student funding in nine states — Alabama, Arizona, Idaho, Illinois, Kentucky, Louisiana, New Hampshire, Pennsylvania, and South Carolina — is down by more than 30 percent since the start of the recession.
- In 12 states, per-student funding fell over the last year. Of these, four states — Arkansas, Illinois, Kentucky, and Vermont — have cut per-student higher education funding for the last two consecutive years.
- In the last year, 38 states increased funding per student. Per-student funding rose $199, or 2.8 percent, nationally.

Deep state funding cuts have had major consequences for public colleges and universities. States (and to a lesser extent localities) provide roughly 54 percent of the costs of teaching and instruction at these schools. Schools have made up the difference with tuition increases, cuts to educational or other services, or both.

Since the recession took hold, higher education institutions have:

- Increased tuition. Public colleges and universities across the country have increased tuition to compensate for declining state funding and rising costs. Annual published tuition at four-year public colleges has risen by $2,333, or 33 percent, since the 2007-08 school year. In Arizona, published tuition at four-year schools is up nearly 90 percent, while in six other states — Alabama, California, Florida, Georgia, Hawaii, and Louisiana — published tuition is up more than 60 percent.

- These sharp tuition increases have accelerated longer-term trends of college becoming less affordable and costs shifting from states to students. Over the last 20 years, the price of attending a four-year public college or university has grown significantly faster than the median income. Although federal student aid and tax credits have risen, on average they have fallen short of covering the tuition increases.
- Diminished academic opportunities and student services. Tuition increases have compensated for only part of the revenue loss resulting from state funding cuts. Over the past several years, public colleges and universities have cut faculty positions, eliminated course offerings, closed campuses, and reduced student services, among other cuts.

A large and growing share of future jobs will require college-educated workers. Sufficient public investment in higher education to keep quality high and tuition affordable, and to provide financial aid to students who need it most, would help states develop the skilled and diverse workforce they will need to compete for these jobs.

Sufficient public investment can only occur, however, if policymakers make sound tax and budget decisions. State revenues have improved significantly since the depths of the recession but are still only modestly above pre-recession levels. To make college more affordable and increase access to higher education, many states need to supplement that revenue growth with new revenue to fully make up for years of severe cuts.

But just as the opportunity to invest is emerging, lawmakers in a number of states are jeopardizing it by entertaining tax cuts that in many cases would give the biggest breaks to the wealthiest taxpayers. In recent years, states such as Wisconsin, Louisiana, and Arizona have enacted large-scale tax cuts that limit resources available for higher education. And in Illinois and Pennsylvania ongoing attempts to find necessary resources after large tax cuts threaten current and future higher education funding.

States Have Reversed Some Funding Cuts, but They Must Do Much More

State and local tax revenue is a major source of support for public colleges and universities. Unlike private institutions, which rely more heavily on charitable donations and large endowments to help fund instruction, public two- and four-year colleges typically rely heavily on state and local appropriations. In 2015, state and local dollars constituted 54 percent of the funds these institutions used directly for teaching and instruction.

While states have begun to restore funding, resources are well below what they were in 2008 — 18 percent per student lower — even as state revenues have returned to pre-recession levels. In the states that have finalized their higher education budgets for the current 2015-16 school year compared with the 2007-08 school year, when the recession hit, adjusted for inflation:

- State spending on higher education nationwide is down an average of $1,598 per student, or 18 percent.
- In only four states — Montana, North Dakota, Wisconsin, and Wyoming — is per-student funding now above its 2008 pre-recession levels.
- 26 states have cut funding per student by more than 20 percent.
- Nine states have cut funding per student by more than 30 percent.
- Arizona and Illinois have cut funding by more than half.

Over the past year, most states increased per-student funding for their public higher education systems. Thirty-eight states are investing more per student in the 2015-16 school year than they did in 2014-15.

- Nationally, spending is up an average of $199 per student, or 2.8 percent.
- The funding increases vary from $13 per student in Missouri to $1,730 in Wyoming.

- 15 states increased per-student funding by more than 5 percent.
- Five states — Colorado, Nevada, Oregon, Washington, and Wyoming — increased funding by more than 10 percent: But this trend is far from universal. In 12 states, per-student funding *fell* over the last year — declining, on average, 8.8 percent or by more than $516 per student.
- Funding cuts vary from $20 per student in New Jersey to $1,746 in Illinois.
- Six states — Alaska, Arizona, Illinois, Oklahoma, West Virginia, and Wisconsin — cut funding by more than $250 per student over the past year.
- Four states — Arkansas, Illinois, Kentucky, and Vermont — have cut per-student higher education funding for the last two years.

After the Recession, States Cut Higher Education Funding as Enrollment Rose

Reductions in support for public colleges reflect in part the strategy that many states chose during the deep national recession and slow recovery.

- State tax revenues fell sharply during the Great Recession. The recession of 2007-09 led to record-breaking declines in state revenues, and the slow recovery continues to affect them. High unemployment and a slow recovery in housing values left people with less income and less purchasing power. As a result, states took in less from income tax and sales tax, their main sources of revenue for funding education and other services. By the fourth quarter of 2015, eight years after the recession hit, total state tax revenues were just 6.4 percent greater than they were at the start of the recession after adjusting for inflation.

- Many states chose to close their budget deficits through sizeable budget cuts rather than a more balanced mix of spending reductions and revenue increases. States relied disproportionately on damaging cuts to deal with declining revenue over the course of the recession. Between fiscal years 2008 and 2012, states made up 45 percent of the loss in revenue through reducing support for public services — and only 16 percent through increases in taxes and fees. (They closed the remainder of their shortfalls with federal aid, reserves, and various other measures.) States would have lessened the deep cuts to higher education if they had been more willing to raise additional revenue.
- Meanwhile, college enrollment has risen. Public higher education institutions must educate more students, raising costs. Enrollment in public higher education was up by nearly 900,000 full-time-equivalent students, or 8.6 percent, between the beginning of the recession and the 2013-14 academic year (the latest year for which there are actual data).
- The recession played a large role in swelling enrollment numbers, particularly at community colleges, as many high school graduates chose college over dim employment prospects and older workers returned to retool and gain new skills.
- Other areas of state budgets also are under pressure. For example, an estimated 803,000 more K-12 students are enrolled in the current school year than in 2008. Long-term growth in state prison populations — with state facilities now housing nearly 1.56 million inmates — also continues to put pressure on state spending.

State Cuts Have Helped Drive Up Tuition

In recent years states have modestly increased investment in two- and four-year colleges from their recession lows. As such, tuition hikes have been much smaller than they were in the worst years of the recession. Published tuition — the "sticker price" — at public four-year institutions increased in 34 states over the past year, but only modestly. Average tuition increased $254, or 2.8 percent. Between last year and this year:

- Louisiana increased average tuition across its four-year institutions more than any other state, hiking it by more than 7 percent, or roughly $540.
- Nine states raised average tuition by more than 5 percent.
- In Washington State, tuition actually fell by nearly 4 percent.

Nevertheless, tuition remains much higher than it was before the recession in most states. Since the 2007-08 school year, average annual published tuition has risen by $2,333 nationally, or 33 percent. Steep tuition increases have been widespread, and average tuition at public four-year institutions, has increased by:

- more than 60 percent in seven states;
- more than 40 percent in 14 states; and
- more than 20 percent in 39 states.

In Arizona, the state with the greatest tuition increases since the recession hit, tuition has risen 87.8 percent, or $4,978 per student. Average tuition at a four-year Arizona public university is now $10,646 a year.

Public Colleges and Universities Also Have Cut Staff and Eliminated Programs

Tuition increases, while substantial in most states, have fallen far short nationally of fully replacing the per-student support that public colleges and universities have lost due to state funding cuts. In nearly half of the states, tuition increases between 2008 and 2015 have not fully offset cuts to state higher education funding.

Because tuition increases have not fully compensated for the loss of state funding, and because most public schools do not have significant endowments or other sources of funding, many public colleges and universities have simultaneously reduced course offerings, student services, and other campus amenities.

Data on spending at public institutions of higher learning in recent years are incomplete, but considerable evidence suggests that these actions by many public colleges and universities likely reduced the quality and availability of their academic offerings. For example, since the start of the recession, colleges and university systems in some states have eliminated administrative and faculty positions (in some instances replacing them with non-tenure-track staff), cut courses or increased class sizes, and in some cases, consolidated or eliminated whole programs, departments, or schools.

Public colleges and universities continue to make these types of cuts, even as states have begun to reinvest in higher education. For example:

- The University of Alaska Fairbanks eliminated six degree offerings — including engineering management, science management, and philosophy.
- The University of Arizona cut 320 positions from its budget including layoffs, firings, and resignations, and increased class sizes for core undergraduate courses.
- In addition to laying off over 200 employees the University of Akron in Ohio eliminated its school baseball team.
- Facing large state funding cuts, the University of Wisconsin-Madison laid off or reduced staff and faculty vacancies by 400 slots and held faculty salaries level.

Nationwide, employment at public colleges and universities has grown modestly since the start of the recession, but proportionally less than the growth in the number of students. Between 2008 and 2014, the number of full-time-equivalent instructional staff at public colleges and universities grew by about 7 percent, while the number of students at these institutions grew by 8.6 percent. In other words, the number of students per faculty member rose nationwide.

Funding Cuts and Tuition Increases Have Shifted Costs from States to Students

Over time, students have assumed much greater responsibility for paying for public higher education. That's because during and immediately following recessions, state and local funding for higher education has tended to fall, while tuition has tended to grow more quickly. During periods of economic growth, funding has tended to recover somewhat while tuition has stabilized at a higher level as a share of total higher educational funding.

In 1988, public colleges and universities received 3.2 times as much revenue from state and local governments as they did from students. They now receive about 1.2 times as much from states and localities as from students.

Nearly every state has shifted costs to students over the last 25 years — with the most drastic shift occurring since the onset of the Great Recession. In 1988, average tuition amounts were larger than per-student state expenditures in only two states, New Hampshire and Vermont. By 2008, that number had grown to ten states. In 2015 (the latest year for which there is data), tuition revenue was greater than state and local government funding for higher education in 22 states, with six — Colorado, Delaware, Michigan, New Hampshire, Pennsylvania, and Vermont — requiring students and families to shoulder higher education costs by a ratio of at least 2-to-1.

Families Have Been Hard-Pressed to Absorb Rising Tuition Costs

The cost shift from states to students has happened over a period when absorbing additional expenses has been difficult for many families because their incomes have been stagnant or declining. In the 1970s and early- to mid-1980s, tuition and incomes both grew modestly faster than inflation; by the late 1980s, tuition began to rise much faster than incomes.

- Since 1973, average inflation-adjusted public college tuition has increased by 274 percent while median household income has grown by only 7 percent.
- Over the past 40 years, the incomes of the top 1 percent of families have grown by almost 170 percent. This means that public college tuition has outpaced income growth for even the highest earners.
- The sharp tuition increases states have imposed since the recession have exacerbated the longer-term trend. Tuition jumped nearly 30 percent between the 2007-08 and 2014-15 school years, while real median income fell roughly 6.5 percent over the same time period.

Cost Shift Harms Students and Families, Especially Those With Low Incomes

Rapidly rising tuition at a time of weak or declining income growth has damaging consequences for families, students, and the national economy.

- Tuition costs deter some students from enrolling in college. While the recession encouraged many students to enroll in higher education, the large tuition increases of the past few years may have prevented further enrollment gains. Rapidly rising tuition makes it less likely that students will attend college. Research has consistently found that college price increases result in declining enrollment. While many universities and the federal government provide financial aid to help students bear the price, research suggests that a high sticker price can dissuade students from enrolling even if the net price, including aid, doesn't rise.
- Rising tuition may be harming students of color and reducing campus diversity. New research finds that rising tuition and fees jeopardize campus diversity at public four-year colleges as students of color are less likely to enroll as the cost of tuition goes up. "All else equal, a $1,000 tuition increase

for full-time undergraduate students is associated with a drop in campus diversity of almost 6 percent," New York University researchers found in a 2015 study. Another study, which examined tuition policy changes in Texas in the early 2000s, concluded that rising tuition rates limited enrollment gains for Hispanic students in the state. The share of students coming from communities of color at public two- and four-year colleges had risen significantly in the years leading up to these tuition increases. State cuts to higher education, made up for with higher tuition rates, jeopardize this trend.

- Tuition increases likely deter low-income students, in particular, from enrolling. College cost increases have the biggest impact on students from low-income families, research further shows. For example, a 1995 study by Harvard University researcher Thomas Kane concluded that states with the largest tuition increases during the 1980s and early 1990s "saw the greatest widening of the gaps in enrollment between high- and low-income youth." The relative lack of knowledge among low-income families about the admissions and financial aid process may exacerbate these damaging effects. Students from families that struggle to get by — including those who live in communities with lower shares of college-educated adults and attend high schools that have higher student-to-counselor ratios — tend to overestimate the true cost of higher education more than students from wealthier households in part because they are less aware of the financial aid for which they are eligible.

- These effects are particularly concerning because gaps in college enrollment between higher- and lower-income youth are *already* pronounced. In 2012, just over half of recent high school graduates from families with income in the lowest 20 percent enrolled in some form of postsecondary education, as opposed to 82 percent of students from the top 20 percent. Significant enrollment gaps based on income exist even among prospective students with similar academic records and test scores. Rapidly rising costs at public colleges and universities may widen these gaps further.

- Tuition increases may be pushing lower-income students toward less-selective public institutions, reducing their future earnings. Perhaps just as important as a student's decision to enroll in higher education is the choice of which college to attend. A large share of high-achieving students from struggling families fail to apply to any selective colleges or universities, a 2013 Brookings Institution study found. Even here, research indicates that financial constraints and concerns about cost push lower-income students to narrow their list of potential schools and ultimately enroll in less-selective institutions. Another 2013 study found evidence that some high-achieving, low-income students are more likely to "undermatch" in their college choice in part due to financial constraints.

- Where a student decides to go to college has broad economic implications, especially for economically disadvantaged students and students of color. Students who had parents with less education, as well as African American and Latino students, experienced higher postgraduate earnings by attending more elite colleges relative to similar students who attended less-selective universities, a 2011 study by Stanford University and Mathematica Policy Research found.

Federal Financial Aid Is Up Since the Recession but State Aid Is Down

As tuition soared after the recession, federal financial aid also increased. The Federal Pell Grant Program — the nation's primary source of student grant aid — increased the amount of aid it distributed by just over 80 percent between the 2007-08 and 2014-15 school years. This substantial boost has enabled the program not only to reach more students — 2.7 million more students received Pell support last year than in 2008 — but also to provide the average recipient with more support. The average grant rose by 21 percent — to $3,673 from $3,028.

The increase in federal financial aid has helped many students and families cover recent tuition hikes. The College Board calculates that the annual value of grant aid and higher education tax benefits for students at four-year public colleges nationally has risen by an average of $1,410 in real terms since the 2007-08 school year, offsetting about 61 percent of the average $2,320 tuition increase. For community colleges, increases in student aid have more than made up the difference, leading to a drop in net tuition for the average student.

Since the sticker-price increases have varied so much from state to state while federal grant and tax-credit amounts are uniform across the country, students in states with large tuition increases ¾ such as Arizona, Georgia, and Louisiana ¾ likely still experienced substantial increases in their net tuition and fees, while the net cost for students in states with smaller tuition increases may have fallen.

Financial aid provided by *states*, however — which was far less than federal aid even before the recession — has *fallen* on average. In the 2007-2008 school year, state grant dollars equaled $740 per student. By 2014, the latest year for which full data is available, that number had fallen to $710, a drop of roughly 4 percent.

[...]

Federal Budget Deficits Do Not Indicate That the Federal Government Is Ineffective

Robert Eisner

Robert Eisner was an American author and professor of economics at Northwestern University. He was recognized throughout the United States for his expertise and knowledge of macroeconomics and the economics of business cycles.

Almost everybody talks about federal budget deficits. Almost everybody is against them in principle. And almost no one knows what he or she is talking about.

Maybe it goes back to something deep in our Calvinist heritage, that we must suffer rather than borrow. "No gain without pain," goes the modern version. We must raise taxes or cut useful govern- for a better future.

Or perhaps it has more recent political roots. Franklin D. Roosevelt pledged but never managed to "balance the budget," and Republicans attacked Democrats over budget deficits for the next 50 years. Then, with the huge Reagan-era deficits, Democrats thought they had their chance and turned the tables on the issue. In charting his independent course, Ross Perot has made the deficit his principal issue and has advanced a number of extreme "solutions" to the problem, including a balanced-budget amendment to the Constitution. President Clinton, in his initial State of the Union address on the economy, was constrained to present a comprehensive deficit reduction package.

The public has always agreed in wide proportions that the deficit should be eliminated. But it is far from clear that any candidate—Republican, Democrat, or Independent—has ever won an election with this position. In fact, many have lost by opposing popular deficit-increasing measures or by supporting tax increases

"Sense and Nonsense About Budget Deficits," by Robert Eisner, Harvard Business School Publishing, May-June 1993. Reprinted by permission.

constitutions to balance their current or operating budgets, finance capital outlays (like roads and bridges and new water systems or school buildings) separately, by borrowing.

Even this, however, would not now do much for the federal government deficit. Assume, counter-factually, that federal accounting conformed to private business practice and included in the budget only the depreciation on past tangible investment, not current tangible capital investment. The resulting U.S. federal budget deficit would be virtually the same as the overall deficits generally reported. This is a manifestation of something of which we should be much more aware—virtually zero net public investment in physical infrastructure. Our public physical plant is wearing out at least as fast as it is being replaced. A more comprehensive measure of investment, though, would include the OMB's estimates of "Major Federal Capital Outlays" for research and development and education and training as well as physical capital. If we used this measure, net investment, reflecting (however inadequately) the needs of our growing population, would be positive. Its exclusion would reduce the measure of the deficit by perhaps $80 billion of the $290 billion reported for our last fiscal year.

Given some $175 billion per year of federal grants to state and local governments, it might make some sense to present a consolidated account for all of government, as the U.S. Bureau of Economic Analysis does in its national income and product accounts. If we do that and then separate out all capital expenditures, for both tangible and intangible investment, we find that while the total consolidated 1991 budget retains a deficit of $193 billion, the current account portion of that deficit is only $24 billion.

A large part of the deficit is accountable directly to our slow economy and high unemployment. The U.S. Congressional Budget Office indeed estimates that each percentage point of unemployment adds, in the short term, $50 billion to the deficit, with the amount growing over time as additional deficit adds more to debt and subsequent interest payments.

If national unemployment in 1993 were merely back at its 5.3% average of the years 1988 to 1990—instead of hovering at nearly 7%—the deficit would be $100 billion less; by 1996, as a consequence of interest payment savings on a lesser accumulated debt, it would be some $130 billion less. Virtually all of the Clinton-Gore Administration's commitment to deficit reduction could be realized by that minimal reduction in unemployment. Achieving a 4% unemployment rate, which has long been a target, or a 3% rate such as during the Vietnam War, could bring about an even greater reduction in the deficit.

The Office of Management and Budget, in its final document released by President Bush, offered "baseline" deficit estimates grounded on the relatively pessimistic economic outlook of 51 private "blue chip" forecasters. They foresaw real GDP growth of only 3% in 1993, 2.9% in 1994, and then down to 2.5% from 1995 to 1998; unemployment was still projected at 5.7% for 1998.

The OMB also presented deficit estimates on the basis of "high-growth" projections, which had the GDP increasing in successive years at 3.5%, 4.0%, 3.7%, 3.4%, 3.2%, and 3.0%, with unemployment down to 5.0% in 1998, its level in March, 1989 at the beginning of the Bush Administration. I have added estimates of what the deficit would have been in any year over which unemployment had averaged 5%. These were calculated on the assumption, consistent with Congressional Budget Office calculations, that each percentage point reduction in unemployment is associated in the short run, without including eventual interest savings, with a reduction in the deficit equal to 0.8% of the GDP.

I have compared deficit projections under the different assumptions as to growth and employment, and the results are striking. With no additional spending cuts or tax increases, the deficit would have fallen, in the high-growth scenario, from 4.9% of the GDP in 1992 to 2.1% in 1998, more than meeting the Clinton Administration's goals. If unemployment had been down to 5% throughout the period, instead of just in any given year, there would have been growing interest savings on a lower debt, and the deficit would have shrunk even more than shown in my short-run 5% unemployment curves.

The Deficit in a Growing Economy

In an expanding economy with an increasing population, almost everything grows: births and deaths, marriages and divorces, borrowing and repayment, income and wealth, and assets and debt. The criterion for increasing debt—how much borrowing there should be—is directly related to income. This is true for the government as well as for prudent private borrowers, banks, and businesses. Governments, as well as people, should not indefinitely allow their debt to grow faster than their income.

One may well argue that a responsible deficit target, similar to responsible targets for private business and households, is that debt over the long run grow no faster than income or, for the nation, gross domestic product (GDP). At the end of the 1939 fiscal year, as the New Deal was giving way to World War II, the gross federal debt held by the public came to $41 billion, 47% of GDP. In 1946, after World War II, it reached $242 billion, or 114% of GDP. By 1980, with federal budget deficits in all of the years from 1961 on, the debt had grown to $709 billion, but had fallen, relatively, to 27% of GDP. At the end of the 1992 fiscal year, the debt held by the public was $2,999 billion, up to 51% of GDP, but still only a little more than it was in 1939 and less than half of its proportion just after World War II. We may note both the short-period changes and the secular swings of the debt-GDP ratio in the graph "Some Say to Watch the Debt-GDP Ratio."

There is nothing sacrosanct about any particular debt-GDP ratio. In periods of recession we may expect deficits to rise and the debt to grow more rapidly than GDP, which will itself be growing much less rapidly, if at all. If there is need for major investment, debt may again grow faster than GDP.

But suppose we were to keep the debt-GDP ratio constant. It is instructive to note what this "equilibrium" target would imply for our current situation. If we maintained the approximate 1992 debt-

GDP ratio of 0.5 and assumed an estimated 7% growth, then the projected 1993 deficit would be $210 billion. Compare this with the final Bush OMB projected 1993 deficit of $327 billion as well as with the $227 billion that deficit would be if unemployment were two percentage points less.

The Bush OMB's final deficit projections are based on the "blue chip" private forecasters' anticipation of an unemployment rate averaging 7.2% for all of calendar 1993! Greeted with much expression of concern, the OMB had its mismeasured deficit declining from $327 billion in 1993 to $270 billion in 1994 and $230 billion in 1995 before beginning to rise again to $266 billion in 1996, $305 billion in 1997, and $320 billion in 1998. They assumed unemployment above 6% through 1995 and at 5.7% in 1998. The OMB also assumed interest rates on 91-day Treasury bills would rise, unaccountably, from their current rate of less than 3% to over 5%, thus adding perhaps another $50 billion to the annual deficit.

Those projections, though, even if correct, would still have the deficit-to-GDP ratio below 3.9%, with the debt-GDP ratio virtually stable, at 57%, by 1998. The debt would then be growing at a 6.67% per annum rate with a projected nominal GDP growth of 5.93%. If the rate of growth of GDP were over 6.67%, the debt-GDP ratio would be declining. If unemployment were down only to its 5.2% rate of 1989 and Treasury bill rates were still around 3%, the resulting 1997 deficit would be not $305 billion but on the order of $200 billion, or 2.5% of GDP. With a slightly more ambitious 7% rate of growth of GDP, the debt-GDP ratio would then be headed for an equilibrium ratio of 36%, well below its current figure of about 51%. In a meaningful, relative sense, President Clinton would have reduced "our massive debt."

How Do Deficits Hurt? Or Do They?

Much of what is written and said about the damage done by federal budget deficits is sheer nonsense, no matter how often repeated. First, of course, the notion that the federal government will go bankrupt because it is unable to pay off or service its debt is absurd.

A sovereign government need never overtly repudiate a debt in its own currency. It can always tax those subject to its laws, including bondholders, to get the necessary proceeds. Or it can simply print the money needed—in the case of the United States, have the Federal Reserve buy Treasury securities. That may have other consequences, which we will consider. But in any event, there is no issue of bankruptcy for debt in dollars. (Debt denominated in a foreign currency, which is not the case for the United States, is quite another matter.) The debt may be repaid in cheaper dollars, but there is no reason why it cannot be repaid.

Ross Perot warned repeatedly that we are "spending our children's money." But our children's money has not yet been printed and will of course be printed or supplied when our children need it, in whatever quantities the interaction of the monetary authorities and our banking and financial system then determine. Alan Greenspan's successors in the Federal Reserve will always be able to supply money for our children. What they cannot supply and, we shall see, what may be lacking are the real resources of capital—public and private, tangible and intangible, human and nonhuman—with which we are failing now to endow our children.

We are also told that our continuing deficits mean we are passing ever greater debt on to our children. This is literally true. Our children will be the *owners* of all those Treasury bills, notes and bonds that constitute the debt. That will give them a nice cushion of accumulated savings. Is that necessarily so bad?

We are further told that the interest burden of the debt, currently about $185 billion per year, is a heavy drag on the economy. In fact it comes to only about 3% of GDP. But, more fundamentally, the interest payments of the Treasury are, after all, income to their recipients. Any taxes that may be levied to finance the payments are then matched by added income.

There are those who call this a regressive redistribution of income, on the assumption that the rich receive interest income financed by taxes paid by the poor. A moment's reflection casts major doubt on that assumption. The ultimate beneficiaries of the interest receipts—via pension funds, insurance, and banking services, as well as savings bonds—must for the most part be in the large middle class. And relatively little is paid in taxes by the very poor. The social cost of debt and deficits will have to be found elsewhere.

On a more sophisticated level, some might argue that if marginal tax rates are three percentage points higher to finance interest payments, work-effort may be discouraged. People receiving large proportions of their income in the form of interest would not wish to work to earn more with Uncle Sam taking still another three cents out of every additional dollar. But with interest income only 3% of GDP (a bit higher as a percentage of national income), we are a long way from having to worry about that.

It is also said that large deficits will cause inflation. The first answer to this is that we have had some large deficits in the last decade, and inflation has declined sharply. It is running currently at no more than 3% by official measure and is probably less, perhaps zero with full adjustment for product improvement. Indeed, the times series relation between deficits and inflation in the United States has generally been negative; bigger deficits have come with less inflation and smaller deficits with more inflation. To be fair, however, this reflects primarily the effect of the economy on the deficit, rather than the deficit on the economy. In recessions, inflation tends to be less, and, with lesser tax revenues and greater outlays for unemployment benefits, deficits are larger. In booms, inflation may be more while tax revenues are greater and unemployment benefits less, so that deficits are less.

An appropriate test of the effect of deficits on inflation, or on any other economic variables, would have then to abstract from the reverse effect of those variables on the deficit. One way to get at this is to work with a measure of the deficit that is not affected by the fluctuations of the economy. For this purpose we may use what has variously been called the structural, the cyclically-adjusted, or the "high-employment" budget. This indicates what tax revenues, outlays, and the deficit *would* be if the economy were on some fixed path as, say, a 6% unemployment path for a measure that has been published periodically by the Bureau of Economic Analysis. The size of the high-employment deficit may then be a measure of fiscal stimulus. But larger high-employment deficits have also not been associated with more inflation.

The reason for this negative finding brings us closer to the fundamental relation of government deficits and government debt to the economy. That depends very considerably on the state of the economy, whether it is zooming along at top speed or is in a sluggish, slack-resources, unemployment mode. Recognizing this will lead us to the conclusion, however shocking to some, that *deficits can be good for us.* This is not to say that they are always beneficial, but they will be good if they generate otherwise lacking purchasing power for the products of American business. In general, deficits can be too small as well as too large. And for most of the past half-century, including right now, contrary to the conventional wisdom, we will find that deficits have been too small. Far from struggling to reduce the deficit, as President Clinton has constrained himself, or offering demagogic appeals for zero deficits (or even surpluses to "pay off" the debt), as has Mr. Perot, we should be looking for the most productive ways to increase it.

Are Deficits Irrelevant?

There is a school of thought, led by Harvard's Robert Barro, which argues that deficits essentially do not matter. This is not my argument. What Barro and his many followers (still a minority among economists) claim is that financing government expenditures by borrowing and by taxes (at least nondistortionary "lump-sum" ones) are equivalent in their effects on the economy. This proposition is called "Ricardian equivalence," after the great classical economist, David Ricardo, who first suggested the possibility before later rejecting it. It reasons that if taxpayers have greater aftertax incomes because government expenditures are financed by borrowing instead of by taxes, they will not spend their extra income. Instead, they will save it to pay the future taxes necessary to service the resulting debt, or else leave the money to their children, who will pay those taxes.

The arguments against Ricardian equivalence are myriad: the difference between borrowing and lending costs of government and private agents who frequently have liquidity constraints; the lack of certainty or even knowledge by any of us that taxes will in fact be higher in the foreseeable future or that others, including the parents of our children's spouses or the other grandparents of our grandchildren, will not pay those taxes; and finally the case where we have no children or else consider them worthless and not worth providing for. But I leave that debate to the economics journals, which have filled many pages with it.

[...]

CHAPTER 3

Is the Federal Government Vital in Preventing States from Taking Unjust or Unwise Action?

State Budgets Are Treated Differently Than the Federal Budget

National Conference of State Legislatures

The National Conference of State Legislatures helps states remain strong and independent by giving them the tools, information, and resources to craft the best solutions to difficult problems.

Requirements that states balance their budgets are often said to be a major difference between state and federal budgeting. State officials certainly take an obligation to balance the budget seriously, and in the debate over a federal balanced budget in the early- and mid-1990s, much of the discussion centered on the states' with balanced budgets. This article is concerned with the nature, definition and enforcement of state balanced-budget requirements.

Nature of State Balanced-Budget Requirements

All the states except Vermont have a legal requirement of a balanced budget. Some are constitutional, some are statutory, and some have been derived by judicial decision from constitutional provisions about state indebtedness that do not, on their face, call for a balanced budget. The General Accounting Office has commented that "some balanced budget requirements are based on interpretations of state constitutions and statutes rather than on an explicit statement that the state must have a balanced budget."

The requirements vary in stringency from state to state. In some states the requirement is that the introduced budget be balanced, or that the enacted budget be balanced. In other states policymakers are required to ensure that expenditures in a fiscal year stay within the cash available for that fiscal year.

"State Balanced Budget Requirements," National Conference of State Legislatures, April 12, 1999. © National Conference of State Legislatures. Reprinted by permission.

Other states may carry unavoidable deficits into the next fiscal year for resolution.

There are three general kinds of state balanced budget requirements:

- The governor's proposed budget must be balanced (43 states and Puerto Rico).
- The budget the legislature passes must be balanced (39 states and Puerto Rico).
- The budget must be balanced at the end of a fiscal year or biennium, so that no deficit can be carried forward (37 states and Puerto Rico).

Such provisions can be either constitutional and statutory, but are more rigorous if they are constitutional since they are not subject to legislative amendment. Some states have two or all three of the possible balanced-budget requirements, and a few have only a statutory requirement that the governor submit a balanced budget. Weighing such considerations against one another, one federal study concluded that 36 states have rigorous balanced-budget requirements, four have weak requirements, and the other 10 fall in between those categories.

What Has to Be Balanced?

State balanced budget requirements in practice refer to operating budgets and not to capital budgets. Operating budgets include annual expenditures—such items as salaries and wages, aid to local governments, health and welfare benefits, and other expenditures that are repeated from year to year. State capital expenditure, mainly for land, highways, and buildings, is largely financed by debt. Court decisions and referendums on borrowing have led to the exclusion of expenditures funded by long-term debt from calculations whether a budget is balanced.

In practice, the following kinds of state revenues and expenditures also have little impact on state balanced budgets:

- Almost all federal reimbursements or grants to a state are committed to specific purposes, and the governor and legislature have little discretion over the use of most federal funds.
- Transportation trust fund money raised from state motor fuel taxes is usually earmarked for highways and other transportation purposes.
- Some tax collections may be diverted to local governments or other specified purposes without appropriations.
- Some states allow agencies or programs to collect and spend fees, charges or tuition without annual or biennial appropriations.

In each case, it is practically impossible for revenues and expenditures to get out of balance, since expenditures are controlled by available funds.

Thus it is not surprising that the focus of "balancing the budget" tends to be on the general fund although general fund expenditures compose only 50 percent to 60 percent of total state spending.

Enforcement of Balanced Budget Requirements

State requirements for balanced budgets do not impose legal penalties for failure to do so. There are, however, two sorts of enforcement mechanisms. Prohibitions against carrying deficits into the next fiscal year and restrictions on the issuance of state debt help to enforce balanced budget provisions by making it difficult to finance a deficit. In many states governors or joint legislative-executive commissions can revise budgets after they are enacted to bring them into balance.

Unlike the federal government, states are not able to issue debt routinely. Issues of general obligation debt require at least the approval of the legislature and in many states, voter approval. The issue of revenue bonds requires legislation to create an agency to issue bonds and the creation of a revenue stream to repay the debt. These practices mean that the issuance of debt is fully in the public view. It is extremely rare for a state government to borrow long-term funds to cover operating expenses, although. Louisiana did in 1988 and Connecticut did in 1991. There do not appear to be any other examples of this practice from recent years.

A legislature and governor can jointly revise a budget at any time. But most legislatures are not in session throughout the year, and some legislatures meet only for a few months every other year. Requiring legislative consent for every change in a budget would impose delays or the costs of special sessions. Therefore, many state constitutions allow governors or special commissions to revise budgets after they have been enacted to bring expenditures into line with revenues.

Thirty-six states allow governors some degree of authority to reduce spending when it is necessary to maintain a balanced budget, even if enacted budgets call for specific amounts of expenditure. Some states prohibit executive budget revisions, and many restrict the amounts and nature of such reductions. Some states have, in addition, joint legislative and executive boards or commissions that are constitutionally permitted to make budget revisions, for example, to deal with unforeseen revenue shortfalls, emergencies, or unanticipated federal funds.

Practice

State balanced-budget rules are not as rigid as those recommended for the federal government in the early 1990s, which would have forbidden total expenditures above total revenues in any year and would have prohibited new borrowing. By this standard, states routinely run deficits because they borrow to finance capital expenditures. But this does not violate state balanced-budget requirements. Nor does rolling deficits in operating funds forward from one fiscal year to another, if a state constitution permits the practice.

Fiscal stress, however, can induce governors and legislators to adopt expedients so they can observe the letter, if not the spirit, of balanced budget requirements. Among these are sales of state assets, postponing payments to vendors, reducing payments to pension funds, borrowing from one state fund to finance expenditures from another, and "creative" accounting. Such expedients reflect the stress that can arise between legal demands for a balanced budget and political demands for the continuation of state programs without tax increases. The fact that such expedients tend to be limited to times of fiscal stress is in itself a measure of how seriously state elected officials take their responsibility to produce balanced budgets.

How States Fail at Assistance

Liz Schott, Ladonna Pavetti, and Ife Floyd

Liz Schott, Ladonna Pavetti, PhD, and Ife Floyd all work for the Center on Budget and Policy Priorities. Liz Schott currently is a senior fellow with the Center's Welfare Reform and Income Support Division. Ladonna Pavetti is Vice President for Family Income Support Policy. Ife Floyd is a senior policy analyst.

A key feature of the 1996 overhaul of the nation's cash assistance system was turning funding over to the states and giving them broad flexibility on using the funds through the creation of the Temporary Assistance for Needy Families (TANF) block grant. Prior to the TANF block grant, families in need received cash assistance through the Aid to Families with Dependent Children (AFDC) program, under which federal funds matched half or more of every dollar of cash assistance that a state provided to a needy family. A key argument for block granting was that states needed much greater flexibility over the use of the federal funds than AFDC's funding structure provided. Under a block grant, proponents argued, states could shift the funds freed up when families left welfare for work to child care or other work supports, where need would increase. States also could invest more in work programs to reflect the increased emphasis on welfare as temporary and work-focused.

That is not what happened. In TANF's early years, when the economy was strong and cash assistance caseloads were shrinking, states used the flexibility of the block grant to take some of the funds that had gone as benefits to families and redirect them to child care and welfare-to-work programs to further welfare reform efforts. But over time, states redirected a substantial portion of their state and federal TANF funds to other purposes, to fill state

"How States Use Federal and State Funds Under the TANF Block Grant," by Liz Schott, Ladonna Pavetti, PhD, and Ife Floyd, Center on Budget and Policy Priorities, October 15, 2015. http://www.cbpp.org. Reprinted by permission.

budget holes, and in some cases to substitute for existing state spending. Even when need increased during the Great Recession, states were often unable to bring the funds back to core welfare reform services and instead made cuts in basic assistance, child care, and work programs.

Thus, the cash assistance safety net for the nation's poorest families with children has weakened significantly under the TANF block grant, with potentially devastating long-term consequences for children growing up in families with little or no cash income to meet basic needs. And, despite the rhetoric, few of the diverted resources have gone to work preparation or employment for the families. In their recent book, *$2 a Day*, authors Kathryn Edin and Luke Shaefer present a disheartening account of the human impact of states' failure to provide a safety net for families that lose a job or are unable to find work. Instead of the success that some claim welfare reform to be, a close examination of states' use of funds under TANF provides a cautionary tale about the dangers of block-granting core safety-net programs and providing extensive flexibility to states on using the funds.

Currently, states spend *only slightly more than one-quarter* of their combined federal TANF funds and the state funds they must spend to meet TANF's "maintenance of effort" (MOE) requirement on basic assistance to meet the essential needs of families with children, and just *another quarter* on child care for low-income families and on activities to connect TANF families to work. They spend the rest of the funding on other types of services, including programs not aimed at improving employment opportunities for poor families. TANF does not require states to report on whom they serve with the federal or state funds they shift from cash assistance to other uses, let alone what outcomes they achieved. Thus, there is no evidence that giving states this broad flexibility has improved outcomes for poor families with children.

This report examines 2014 spending data to understand spending patterns nationally and to examine the wide variations across states in how TANF/MOE funds are used; fact sheets and the underlying spreadsheet that CBPP issued separately provide state-by-state information. The report's key findings include:

- The share of state and federal TANF spending used for basic assistance (cash welfare grants) has fallen significantly. At TANF's onset, 70 percent of combined federal TANF and state MOE funds went for basic assistance for poor families. By 2014, that figure had plummeted to 26 percent. There is significant variation across states; ten states spent less than 10 percent of their TANF/MOE funds on basic assistance in 2014.

- States spend only about a quarter of their state and federal TANF dollars on child care and work activities combined. A key justification for block-granting TANF was to give states flexibility to move funding from cash assistance to work-related activities and/or supports (such as child care subsidies). States raised spending in these areas in TANF's early years but didn't sustain those modest increases. States used only 8 percent of their TANF and MOE funds for work activities in 2014; ten states spent less than 5 percent. States spent 16 percent of total TANF and MOE funds on child care; 15 states spent less than 5 percent.

- Core welfare reform activities thus represent just half of state and federal TANF spending. Child care, work activities, and basic assistance combined totaled 50 percent of TANF and MOE spending nationally in 2014. The share varied widely across states: eight states spent less than 25 percent of these funds on the three categories, while five states spent more than 75 percent.

- States use a large and growing share of state and federal TANF funds that formerly helped poor families meet their basic needs for other state services. In some cases, states have used TANF and MOE funds to expand programs, such as state Earned Income Tax Credits (EITCs) or pre-K, or to cover the growing costs of existing services, such as child welfare. In other cases, they have used TANF/MOE funds to *replace existing state funds,* thereby freeing those state funds for purposes unrelated to providing a safety net or work opportunities for low-income families.

The extent to which states have used TANF or MOE funds for areas beyond the core welfare reform areas raises serious concerns. TANF's combination of broadly defined purposes and limited accountability for much of its spending has enabled states to divert funds from supporting the poorest families and use them instead to help fill state budget holes. In addition, the annual federal TANF block grant has no adjustment for inflation and thus has eroded badly over time, losing one-third of its value since 1997. These two factors — the funds' diminished value and broadened dispersal — have left states with fewer resources to serve needy families, especially at times of increased need, as the Great Recession and its aftermath showed.

Block grants can weaken accountability and oversight, leading states to spend significant federal funds in ways that Congress did not intend. For many states, the TANF block grant has led to a severe erosion of the cash assistance safety net and very limited fulfillment of the promise that the funds saved would support work.

Background

The TANF block grant fundamentally altered both the structure and the allowable uses of federal and state dollars previously spent on AFDC and related programs. Under TANF, the federal government gives states a fixed block grant totaling $16.5 billion each year. States that meet specified criteria may also qualify for federal "Contingency Funds"; roughly 20 states have done so for the last several years. Under the federal TANF law's MOE requirement, states must maintain a certain level of *state* spending, based on a state's spending for AFDC and related programs prior to TANF's creation in 1996. (States are required to maintain 80 percent, or in some cases 75 percent, of their historic spending level.) In 2014, states spent $31.9 billion in combined federal TANF and state MOE funds, comprising $16.6 billion in federal TANF funds and $15.3 billion in state MOE funds.

States can use their federal TANF dollars and state MOE funds
to support a broad range of activities related to promoting the four
purposes of TANF specified in federal law: (1) assisting needy
families so children can be cared for in their own homes or the
homes of relatives; (2) reducing the dependency of needy parents
by promoting job preparation, work, and marriage; (3) preventing
out-of-wedlock pregnancies; and (4) encouraging the formation
and maintenance of two-parent families.

Reduced Spending on Basic Assistance Has Weakened Safety Net

States spent $8.4 billion of federal TANF and state MOE funds on
basic assistance for poor families in 2014, representing 26 percent
of all TANF and MOE funds spent that year. By contrast, at TANF's
onset, states spent $14 billion on basic assistance, representing
70 percent of combined federal TANF and state MOE funds. While
the strength of each state's safety net and its benefit levels varied
under AFDC, basic assistance represented the single biggest use
of federal and state funds for all states.

The share of state and federal TANF funds spent on basic
assistance varies widely across states, from 6 percent to 61 percent
in 2014. Ten states spent less than 10 percent on basic assistance,
while 11 states spent more than 30 percent. Not surprisingly, the
states that spend the smallest shares of their TANF/MOE funds
on basic assistance generally have lower benefit levels and assist
a smaller share of poor families than the typical state.

California and Texas provide sharp contrasting pictures of
TANF's safety-net role. In both states, the share of poor families
receiving cash assistance has fallen since 1996 and the number of
families in "deep poverty," with incomes below *half* of the poverty
line, has increased. Both states have large populations of poor
families, but the child poverty rate and the share of individuals
who are food insecure are higher in Texas than in California.

California spent 46 percent of its TANF and MOE funds on
basic assistance in 2014. For every 100 poor families with children

in the state, 65 received TANF cash assistance. Monthly benefits for a family of three with no other income were $670 in 2014, or 41 percent of the poverty line. California's food insecurity rate is below the national average.

Texas spent 7 percent of its TANF and MOE funds on basic assistance in 2014. For every 100 poor families with children in the state, 5 received TANF cash assistance. Monthly benefits for a family of three with no other income were $277 in 2014, or 17 percent of the poverty line. Texas' food insecurity rate is above the national average.

Moreover, for families still receiving cash assistance, benefits have plummeted in value in nearly all states — falling 20 percent or more since TANF's creation in 36 states, after adjusting for inflation. Today, in two-thirds of the states, benefits for a family without other cash income now fall below 30 percent of the poverty line; in one-third of the states, benefits are below 20 percent of the poverty line.

Because basic assistance reaches fewer poor families and provides less to those it serves, TANF lifts fewer children out of deep poverty than AFDC did. Nationally, the number of children in deep poverty has risen by nearly 50 percent since the advent of TANF, from 1.5 million to 2.2 million. Also, research suggests that the spending decline on basic assistance has contributed to a rise in "extreme poverty" (defined as income of less than $2 per person per day, a standard that the World Bank uses to measure poverty around the world). Edin and Shaefer find that the number of U.S. households with children living below this $2 threshold has doubled since TANF's creation; among single-parent families, the number has tripled.

Despite Welfare Reform Rhetoric, States Spend Little on Work Activities

A central tenet of TANF is that cash assistance should provide temporary support while a family engages in required activities to help it connect to or prepare for work. Yet most states spend little of their TANF funding on work-related activities. States initially raised spending here somewhat under TANF, but funding has been flat or fallen over the last decade. In 2014, states spent $2.6 billion in TANF and MOE funds on work-related activities, representing 8 percent of total TANF/MOE spending.

As with basic assistance, states vary widely in the share of TANF and MOE spending going to work-related activities, which ranged from 1 percent to 46 percent in 2014. Ten states spent less than 5 percent of their funds in this category, while 12 states spent more than 15 percent (and one state spent more than 40 percent).

Some families receiving these employment or training services may not be receiving cash assistance; for example, this category includes transportation to work for some low-income families that have begun working and ceased receiving (or never received) cash assistance. It also includes wage subsidies, work-related activities, or education and training, some of which goes to low-income families not receiving cash assistance. While this is a permissible use of TANF or MOE funds, it means that some states are investing even less in work programs for cash assistance recipients than the numbers suggest.

Thus, despite the rhetoric of welfare reform — and the fact that many families receiving TANF have significant employment barriers and limited employment prospects — states have withdrawn funding from these activities over most of the last decade. States for the most part are not putting the funds freed up from reduced caseloads into helping TANF recipients prepare for or find work.

Child Care Needs Remain Unmet, Despite Initial Spending Increase

Another central tenet of welfare reform was that states could spend more of the funds on child care to support work, rather than on cash aid. TANF/MOE spending on child care rose dramatically in TANF's early years, from $1.1 billion in 1997 to $5.9 billion in 2000. However, this spending has been flat or declining for over a decade, fluctuating between $5 billion and $6 billion annually. In 2014, states spent $5.1 billion in TANF and MOE funds on child care, representing 16 percent of total TANF/MOE spending.

State spending on child care varies tremendously, ranging from 0 percent to 58 percent of TANF/MOE spending in 2014. Eight states spent more than 30 percent of their TANF/MOE funds on child care, two of which (Delaware and Illinois) spent more than 50 percent. At the other end of the spectrum, 21 states spent less than 10 percent of TANF/MOE funds on child care, nine of which spent less than 3 percent.

In the aftermath of the recession, most states cut child care spending. These cuts reflected more restrictive policies, not less need. While some states have restored some cuts or improved child care subsidy policies in the last couple of years, the improvements have generally been modest; child care assistance continues to reach only a fraction of families in need.

Spending on Working-Family Tax Credits Furthers Welfare Reform Goals

Refundable tax credits for low-income working families are an important work support and a permissible use of TANF and MOE funds. In 2014, 21 states spent a total of $2.6 billion in TANF or MOE funds for refundable tax credits, most commonly a state EITC. This represents 8 percent of national TANF/MOE spending and 16.4 percent of spending for those 21 states. Among those 21 states, the share of TANF/MOE spending going to refundable tax credits ranged from less than 1 percent to 32 percent; in seven states the share exceeded one-fifth.

Refundable state EITCs further the TANF goal of promoting work by helping working families make ends meet and stay employed. They also reduce poverty among working families, with both immediate and long-lasting benefits for children. The availability of TANF or MOE funds may help support enactment (or retention) of a state EITC.

States Spend Relatively Little on Administration and Systems

In 2014, states spent $2.3 billion of TANF/MOE funds on administration and systems, representing 7 percent of total TANF/MOE spending. National spending on administration and systems has been fairly flat under TANF in nominal terms and has declined both in real terms and as a share of total spending. Under federal law, states cannot spend more than 15 percent of TANF funds on administration; most spend far less. While there is some variation across states, this may reflect different state approaches to what costs to include in administration. Variations over time may also reflect significant systems costs that a state incurs for a limited time as a result of computer systems changes.

States Spend One-Third of TANF and MOE Funds in Other Areas

The rest of state and federal TANF spending — nearly $11 billion in 2014, representing one-third of the total — goes to other areas, including child welfare, emergency assistance, early education, teen pregnancy prevention, and marriage support. The share of TANF/MOE spending going to these other areas varies greatly across states, ranging from 4 percent to 80 percent, but exceeds 50 percent in 14 states.

Many, if not all, of the programs and services in these other areas are worthy and important investments. Nonetheless, the question remains whether state and federal TANF funds — rather than other state funds — should be used for them, particularly when the average state spends only around half of its TANF/MOE funding to provide a cash assistance safety net, connect welfare families to work, or provide child care help to low-income working families.

[...]

States Are Responsible for Their Own Fiscal Crises, Not Unfunded Mandates

Brian M. Riedl

Brian Riedl is a senior fellow at the Manhattan Institute and a member of the Manhattan Institute's Economics21, focusing on budget, tax, and economic policy.

States have successfully secured a $20 billion bailout from Washington to close their expanding budget deficits. Never mind that they created their own fiscal crises by increasing spending nearly twice as fast as the federal government has since 1990.

Refusing to accept responsibility for their own reckless spending, states won the media's sympathy by instead blaming a new wave of "unfunded mandates" in education and homeland security imposed on them by Washington.

Now, such mandates are clearly unfair. States should have control over how they spend their own tax dollars — rather than be forced by Washington to fund unwanted programs. Any federal mandate on the states should be accompanied with federal dollars to implement it.

Unfunded mandates, however, didn't cause the current state budget messes.

Only two significant mandates have been enacted since the 1995 Unfunded Mandates Reform Act, according to a new report from the Congressional Budget Office. They are the 1996 minimum-wage increase, and the 1998 limit on federal reimbursements for state food stamp administrative costs. (The funding status of a third mandate, the 2001 port security bill, is still undetermined.) These two mandates cost the states, on average, a combined $9 million per year, or less than one-tenth of 1 percent of most states' general fund. Not exactly a budget-busting amount.

"What Unfunded Mandates?" by Brian M. Riedl, The Heritage Foundation, June 3, 2003. Reprinted by permission.

What about those expensive new education and homeland security programs? Contrary to sympathetic media reports, they're more accurately classified as "programs that states don't want to pay for." An unfunded mandate, after all, must be both unfunded and mandated. And nearly all recent federal education and homeland security programs are either voluntary or fully funded.

Take the No Child Left Behind Act. Washington hasn't mandated that any state implement this law. It merely suggested a model, and offered to subsidize states willing to implement it. States that dislike the federal model, or find the funding insufficient, are free to opt out and run their own programs.

Some call these programs "de facto mandates" because no rational state would opt out of the federal programs. Why is it irrational to opt out? Because the federal money more than justifies the federal strings attached. States enroll unanimously in these programs not because they're required to, but because the deals are too good to pass up.

Then why are states still so angry with Washington? Because they want that money with no strings attached. They've come to consider themselves entitled to the $400 billion they receive annually from Washington. They demand federal dollars, yet they bristle when Congress insists on influencing how its own money is spent.

Consider again the education example. In 1965, Washington offered money to states that volunteered to implement the federal model for educating disadvantaged children. Participating states were given wide latitude to spend this money on their own education programs — latitude states now take for granted. Then, the 2001 No Child Left Behind Act required participating states to more closely align their spending with the program's federal goals. The free lunch of Washington subsidizing states' pet education programs was over.

States may label this reassertion of federal authority over how federal money is spent an "unfunded mandate," but the No Child Left Behind Act is neither unfunded nor mandated. If the program's funding was insufficient to justify the increased federal meddling, states would have opted out. So far, none have.

True, states are still burdened by pre-1996 unfunded mandates. The largest and least fair is Medicaid, whose $200 billion annual cost is only half-funded by Washington. Yet states aren't blameless either, as 60 percent of Medicaid spending is for populations and treatments that states voluntarily added to their own Medicaid programs.

Other pre-1996 unfunded mandates, such as special education and many environmental regulations, should be either funded or removed. But how can states blame 30-year old unfunded mandates for budget crises that suddenly began in 2001?

Note the irony: States demand total control over the spending of their own tax money. Yet by acting as if they're entitled to federal dollars with no strings attached, they challenge Washington's equal right to control how its tax revenues are spent. Now who's trying to impose an unfunded mandate on whom?

States Are More Successful at Addressing Mental Health Concerns

Richard Cauchi

Richard Cauchi is Health Program Director at the National Conference of State Legislatures' (NCSL) Denver office, where he directs projects and research on health finance and costs, health insurance, and pharmaceuticals.

Mental health services have been one significant part of medical care for a number of years. The costs, coverage and availability of such services have been the object of policy discussions and a variety of state legislation. There is not a uniform consensus about the extent to which state government should require coverage for mental health. Since the passage of federal health reform (ACA or PPACA) there is a larger role for the federal government and federal-state coordination, described below. For now, all states and D.C. have some type of enacted law but these laws vary considerably and can be divided roughly into three categories:

Mental Health "Parity" or Equal Coverage Laws

Parity, as it relates to mental health and substance abuse, prohibits insurers or health care service plans from discriminating between coverage offered for mental illness, serious mental illness, substance abuse, and other physical disorders and diseases. In short, parity requires insurers to provide the same level of benefits for mental illness, serious mental illness or substance abuse as for other physical disorders and diseases. These benefits include visit limits, deductibles, copayments, and lifetime and annual limits.

Parity laws contain many variables that affect the level of coverage required under the law. Some state parity laws—such as

Arkansas'—provide broad coverage for all mental illnesses. Other state parity laws limit the coverage to a specific list of biologically based or serious mental illnesses. The state laws labeled full parity below provide equal benefits, to varying degrees, for the treatment of mental illness, serious mental illness and biologically based mental illness, and may include treatment for substance abuse. The newly enacted federal parity law affects insurance policies that already provide some mental health coverage; there is no federal law directly mandating parity to the same extent as state laws; also see background on unsuccessful federal parity legislation below the state table.

Minimum Mandated Mental Health Benefit Laws

Many state laws require that some level of coverage be provided for mental illness, serious mental illness, substance abuse or a combination thereof. They are not considered full parity because they allow discrepancies in the level of benefits provided between mental illnesses and physical illnesses. These discrepancies can be in the form of different visit limits, copayments, deductibles, and annual and lifetime limits. Some mental health advocates believe these laws offer a compromise to full parity that at least provides some level of care. Others feel that anything other than full parity is discrimination against the mentally ill. Some of these laws specify that copayments and deductibles must be equal to those for physical illness up to the required level of benefits provided. If a law does not specify, the copayment could be as much as 50 percent of the cost of the visit and require a separate deductible to be met before mental health visits will be covered.

Mental Health "Mandated Offering Laws"

Mandated offering laws differ from the other two types of laws in that they do not require (or mandate) benefits be provided at all. A mandated offering law can do two things. First, it can require that an option of coverage for mental illness, serious mental illness, substance abuse or a combination thereof, be provided to the insured. This option of coverage can be accepted or rejected and, if accepted, will usually require an additional or higher premium. Second, a mandated offering law can require that if benefits are offered then they must be equal.

Exceptions to Mandate Laws – "Barebones" Policies

Note that some state laws apply primarily to "serious mental illness" and may not assure coverage for particular individual diagnoses or circumstances. Many private market health plans include some type of mental health benefits on a voluntary commercial basis, not necessarily required by state or federal laws. Note that grief counseling may not be considered a covered benefit under some state laws, although it may be offered by insurers as part of a standard mental health benefit package. Laws in at least 38 states include coverage for substance abuse, alcohol or drug addiction.

Mental Health Benefits in the Affordable Care Act (ACA) of 2010

Federal health reform, also termed the PPACA or just ACA, contains a number of provisions which achieve two goals with respect to mental health parity: (1) they expand the reach and applicability of the federal mental health parity requirements; and (2) they create an "essential health benefit" or mandated benefit for the coverage of mental health and substance abuse disorder services in a number of specific insurance financing arrangements. According to a December 2011 report by the Congressional Research Service (CRS), the ACA expands the reach of federal mental health parity requirements to three main types of health plans:

- Qualified health plans as established by the ACA.
- Medicaid non-managed care benchmark and benchmark-equivalent plans.
- Plans offered through the individual market.

The ACA did not alter the federal mental health parity requirements with respect to CHIP plans, but the application of the requirements to CHIP plans, as required in law prior to the

ACA, is explained here in detail. This report also analyzes the impact of the ACA on the existing small employer exemption under federal mental health parity law.

April 2015: Medicaid Rule Proposed On Providing Mental Health 'Parity'

The federal law that passed in 2008 was supposed to ensure that when patients had insurance benefits for mental health and addiction treatment, the coverage was on par with what they received for medical and surgical care. But until 2015, the government had only spelled out how the law applied to commercial plans.

That changed April 7, 2015, when federal officials released a long-awaited rule proposing how the parity law should also protect low-income Americans insured through the government's Medicaid managed care and the Children's Health Insurance Program (CHIP) plans. The proposed regulation is similar to one released in November 2013 for private insurers. "Whether private insurance, Medicaid, or CHIP, all Americans deserve access to quality mental health services and substance use disorder services," said Vikki Wachino, acting director at the Center for Medicaid and CHIP Services.

Federal CMS Guidance Regarding Mental Health Parity Requirements in CHIP, Medicaid and Group Insurance

The Federal Centers for Medicare & Medicaid Services (CMS) issued a State Health Official letter on November 4, 2009 regarding the mental health parity requirements under the Children's Health Insurance Program Reauthorization Act of 2009 (CHIPRA). The letter provides general guidance on implementation of section 502 of CHIPRA, Public Law 111-3, which imposes mental health and substance use disorder parity requirements on all Children's Health Insurance Program (CHIP) State plans under title XXI of the Social Security Act (the Act). This letter also provides preliminary guidance to the extent that mental health and substance use disorder parity requirements apply to State Medicaid programs under title XIX of the Act.

In summary the letter addresses specific requirements in the measure as follows:

1. Qualifying financial requirements and treatment limitations applied to mental health or substance use disorder benefits may be no more restrictive than those applied to medical surgical benefits.

2. No separate qualifying criteria may be applied to mental health or substance use disorder benefits.

3. When out-of-network coverage is available for medical surgical benefits, it must also be available for mental health or substance use disorder benefits.

Medicaid and Group Health Insurance:

Requirements from the Paul Wellstone and Pete Dominici Mental Health Parity and Addiction Equity Act of 2008 (MHPAEA) became effective for group health insurance plans on October 3rd of 2009. These same requirements will only apply to Medicaid insofar as the state's Medicaid agency contracts with one or more managed care organizations (MCOs) or Prepaid Inpatient Health Plans (PIHPs). In these cases the MCOs or PIHPs must be in compliance. A state Medicaid plan is not subject to these requirements otherwise. The MHPAEA applies to all CHIP programs and became effective April 1 of 2009. State CHIP plans are deemed in compliance if they provide coverage of Early and Periodic, Screening, Diagnosis and Treatment (EPSDT) benefits.

States Requiring Legislative Action for Compliance

The letter also specifies that if a state requires legislation in order to be in compliance with the requirements, a state will not be found to be in violation before its next legislative session as long as it notifies the Secretary of HHS and she concurs that legislation is needed. They ask that states in the circumstances submit a letter to the Center for Medicaid and State Operations to that effect as soon as possible and include information as follows:

1. the provisions in question,
2. the reason the state requires legislative action for compliance, and
3. the date the state will begin implementing the provision.

Expanded Mental Health Coverage Rules - November 2013

In a move aimed at boosting mental health treatment, Health and Human Services Secretary Kathleen Sebelius on Nov. 8, 2013 announced new rules that put teeth in the 2008 mental health equity law. The Mental Health Parity and Addiction Equity Act, signed by President George W. Bush, requires doctors and insurers to treat mental illness the same as physical illness. Sebelius made the announcement to applause at the Rosalynn Carter Symposium on Mental Health Policy in Atlanta. The move "finally puts mental health and behavioral health on equal footing," Sebelius said.

On paper, the law made mental health more accessible, but there has been virtually no enforcement of it, said Dr. Jeffrey Lieberman, president of the American Psychiatric Association and a Columbia University psychiatrist. "Up to now, the law has not been complied with," Lieberman said. "Companies have only sort of adhered to it." Insurance companies often cover mental illness in a more limited fashion than physical illness. Now the rule will require insurers to charge similar co-payments regardless if the treatment is for physical or mental health. Deductibles and doctor visits would also be equitable, and there would be parity in outpatient services and residential treatment.

"Many private insurers gave nothing. Some provided benefits, but they were limited and inadequate," Lieberman said. The law, the new rules and provisions of Obamacare combined will ensure mental and physical illness would be covered similarly. America's Health Insurance Plans (AHIP), the professional association that represents the health insurance industry, said it has long supported the act and has worked to implement its requirements in an affordable and effective way.

Federal Parity Amendment

In 1996 a federal parity amendment was signed into law as part of the VA-HUD appropriations bill. The law, otherwise known as the Mental Health Parity Act of 1996 (Public Law 104-204), prohibits group health plans that offer mental health benefits from imposing more restrictive annual or lifetime limits on spending for mental illness than are imposed on coverage of physical illnesses. This law expired on September 30, 2001 due to a "sunset" provision, but was extended through December 31, 2002 when President Bush signed Public Law 107-116. The Mental Health Parity Act of 1996 offers limited parity for the treatment of mental health disorders. The statute does not require insurers to offer mental health benefits, but states that if mental health coverage is offered, the benefits must be equal to the annual or lifetime limits offered for physical health care. It also does not apply to substance use disorders, and businesses with fewer than 26 employees are exempt.

State Laws and Separate Federal Requirements

The state laws noted generally do not apply to federally funded public programs such as Medicaid, Medicare, the Veterans Administration, etc. In addition, "self-funded" health insurance plans, often sponsored by the largest employers, usually are entirely exempt from state regulation because they are preempted by the federal ERISA law.

[...]

Federal Laws Interfere with the LGBTQ Rights Granted by States

Sean Cahill, Mitra Ellen, and Sarah Tobias

Sean Cahill is Director of the National Gay and Lesbian Task Force Policy Institute (NGLTF Policy Institute). Mitra Ellen is an analyst at the NGLFT Policy Institute. Sarah Tobias is a consultant at the NGLTF Policy Institute.

One of the "hottest" issues in the gay, lesbian, bisexual and transgender (GLBT) com- munities today—and in our struggle for equality and liberation—is the issue of family. In the past two decades the GLBT community has experienced a veritable "baby boom." There has been an explosion in the number of organizations created exclusively to serve or advocate on behalf of GLBT families. Same-sex weddings are regular occurrences. Long-standing GLBT organizations of all kinds, including the National Gay and Lesbian Task Force, are doing more and more work in this arena. And legal recognition of our families has become one of the most hotly contested issues on the national, state and local political scenes.

Regardless of sexual orientation or gender identity, our families provide many of the narratives that most profoundly shape each of our lives: love stories of great warmth and joy, eulogies to loss and pain, anecdotes that make us laugh and those that may make us cry. Many of the most passionate stories in art and history take place in a familial set- ting and involve family relationships of all kinds. This is evident from the themes found in Shakespeare and Steinbeck, to the current popularity of TV shows like *Everybody Loves Raymond, Friends, Will & Grace* and *The Sopranos*. More personally, the narratives of family are created through childhood

Cahill, S., Ellen, M., and Tobias, S. (2002). Family Policy: Issues Affecting Gay, Lesbian, Bisexual and Transgender Families. New York: The National Gay and Lesbian Task Force Policy Institute. www.ngltf.org. Reprinted by permission.

and adolescence, through partnership and parenting, through caring for elderly relatives and enjoying our own old age. Our families, however they are comprised, are an important way in which all of us experience and interact with the world.

Just as the stories we tell about family are multifaceted, a concise definition of family is not easy to pin down, especially among those GLBT people who have had to create "families of choice" when they were rejected by their families of origin because of their sexual orientation or gender identity. What is "family" to GLBT people? How are our families different from or the same as those of heterosexual people? While we know that most people define family in terms of relationships rather than technical legal definitions, the sorts of relationships each of us considers to be "family" may differ dramatically. A single parent raising biological or adopted children is a family and so is an elderly, childless couple. A family might also be comprised of adult relatives and friends who cooperate to raise children together. The possibilities are endless.

The debate over the definition of family really becomes heated, of course, when we start to talk about the members of a family in terms of gender identity and sexual orientation. In addition to those examples given above, we define our families as GLBT people co-parenting a child or growing old together. Our definition of family may include transgender parents and bisexuals married to members of the opposite sex or living with same-sex partners. We define family as going far beyond the unit of a married heterosexual couple and their children.

For nearly 20 years there has been much discussion in this country about "culture wars" and the "struggle to define America" (phrases more commonly used by anti-GLBT conservatives). The struggle has ranged from the furor over abortion to prayer in public schools. In addition, GLBT people have found their identities and their families at the center of this maelstrom. Those who seek to define the family solely as a unit constructed around a man married to a woman (as many in the Bush Administration are advocating), thereby excluding GLBT families, single parent families, and many other family structures, are out of step with the reality of today's American family. Their attempt to deny our existence and that of our families is an assault – on our identities, on our families, and on democracy itself.

Why is the definition of family so important? Why is it crucial that our households be included in official definitions of family? What can we do to ensure that our families are protected and included in our society in the same ways as are more traditional families?

These days, some would argue that the "struggle to define America" occurs most often in courtrooms, polling places, council meetings and legislative debates. There are two primary reasons why the definition of family is so important: money and power. We know that when it comes down to the practicalities of daily living, the family unit is a central component of much of the policy and law that govern our lives. Indeed, the definition of the family unit serves as a measure and standard for allocation and distribution of many of the resources and benefits available to citizens (and non-citizens) of this country. And, for those who desire to impose their narrow, exclusionary definition on the rest of us, it serves as an inviolable line they imagine they are holding against the deterioration of the purportedly "moral" America they yearn for— an America without GLBT people, an America without divorce, and an America where women do not work outside the home, among other impossible and archaic notions.

While that "inviolable line" has long fallen, conservatives in this country continue to do everything they can to regain the ground they've lost in promoting a definition of family that is, in fact, irrelevant to most American families. In terms of GLBT families, even a partial list of the ways in which "family policy" discriminates against us is extensive: the tax treatment of same-sex couples, the availability of family-related leave from work, the access to Social Security payments for bereaved same-sex partners, the family-related restrictions written into welfare reform legislation, the custody rights of GLBT parents, policies regarding visiting incarcerated family members, as well as education, health care and immigration policy. Are we seeking to "define America" when we insist upon recognition of the many forms that constitute today's American family, or when we demand that GLBT families be afforded the same rights as those families in which key relationships are heterosexual? Or are we simply seeking a definition that is consistent with one of the most important notions in our democracy: "Life, Liberty and the Pursuit of Happiness?"

On the one hand, we cannot help but be part of this country's definition of family simply by living here, as GLBT partners, parents, and children. On the other hand, if definitions are being scripted without our input, whether in courtrooms or Congress, we must raise our voices and insist on being involved in the process. The Bush Administration has affirmed the family as a priority on the nation's legislative agenda. This priority is being funded heavily through initiatives focusing on marriage and fatherhood, as well as other areas of policy such as welfare and education. How do we ensure that we are among the beneficiaries of new laws and are not being left out or, worse, discriminated against either because of express bigotry or because our families don't fit a narrow, antiquated and inaccurate definition?

Introduction and Executive Summary

Eugene Clark and Larry Courtney lived like many married couples, creating their lives around each other and being recognized by their families and friends as a committed couple. When Larry was offered a job in New York City in 1988, the couple relocated from Washington, D.C. and Eugene found a new position in New York. When New York City created a domestic partnership registry, the couple went to City Hall to get the closest thing to a marriage certificate available to them. And when Eugene's mother became ill, they brought her from D.C. to their one-bedroom Manhattan apartment so that they could care for her during the last years of her life.

On September 11, 2001, Eugene was one of the thousands at the World Trade Center who did not come home to their loved ones that evening. Larry received a voicemail from Eugene after the first building was hit: "Don't worry, the plane hit the other building. I'm okay. We're evacuating." That was the last time Larry heard from him. Like other people who lost family members that day, Larry reported Eugene missing, filled out his death certificate, and, among other things, the workers' compensation forms. However, Larry was informed that since he and Eugene were not legally married, he was not considered family. The compensation would go to Eugene's father with whom Eugene had not spoken in over 20 years.

In the midst of his intense grief, Larry had to counter this claim that he and Eugene were not family, even though they had built a life together for 14 years. Larry joined with Lambda Legal Defense and Education Fund to educate the public, the media and legislators about this unjust situation. On August 20, 2002, the New York State Assembly passed a bill giving the domestic partners of September 11 victims full spousal rights to workers' compensation.

Unfortunately, this type of situation is far from uncommon for same-sex couples and their families. Larry Courtney's predicament was addressed in part because his life partner Eugene was killed in an attack of international significance. Although this was an important victory, most gay, lesbian, bisexual, and transgender (GLBT) families remain routinely discriminated against by public policy. Usually these injustices are not linked to a high profile national tragedy, and these families' stories do not make it to the evening news. Nevertheless, many GLBT people experience personal tragedies—such as the death of a life partner—that are compounded by a callous disregard of their family bonds, and as a result suffer emotionally and economically.

Whether family policy has been created with GLBT people in mind or not, it affects GLBT individuals and influences the security and well being of their families throughout their lives— from childhood through young adulthood, middle age through retirement, and even after death. Much public policy is based on the express goal of promoting "the family," recognizing the economic and emotional interdependence of family members and giving special priority to this bond.

Historically these policies have been based on a narrow definition of family which does not encompass many of the familial bonds of GLBT people. Most policies continue to be gravely lacking in this regard, giving preference to heterosexual married couples and their children over other family formations. Unmarried couples, single parents, extended family caregivers, and the children of these families are all disadvantaged by such policies. Homophobia and heterosexism compound this problem for GLBT families. As a result, the family ties of GLBT people to their children and partners are often ignored, dismissed or attacked. GLBT people are left with little security for their relationships, especially in times of hardship or transition.

In promoting the family unit, one of the stated goals of family policy is to protect the needs of children and to ensure their health and safety.[1] GLBT youth have special needs that can be addressed by public policy. For example, they are at greater risk than other youth of experiencing homelessness, suicide, and violence, and are often unable to find support at school or in their families. In addition, children of GLBT parents are vulnerable to the pervasive homophobia in many schools and communities, and often suffer economic and familial insecurity as a result of the lack of recognition of their ties to their non-biological parents.

As adults, GLBT people continue to be disadvantaged because their families are generally not legally recognized and are often socially disregarded. This can have major repercussions for parents and prospective parents in the arenas of custody and visitation, eligibility to serve as adoptive or foster parents, or eligibility to adopt a partner's child. There can be additional complications for individuals and couples in the arenas of housing, access to social programs and health care, taxation, family leave from work, and rights after the dissolution of a relationship. Finally, GLBT elders face unnecessary hardships because of severe economic penalties, such as ineligibility to receive a deceased partner's Social Security or pension benefits. Other forms of discrimination, such as heterosexist nursing home policies that do not recognize same-sex relationships, also complicate senior GLBT couples' access to services and health care.

[...]

Notes:

1. For example, the "best interest of the child" is the common legal standard used in child welfare decisions, including child placement, custody and visitation. *Finlay v. Finlay* 148 NE 624, 626 (1925) ("[The judge] acts as *parens patriae* to do what is best for the interest of the child.")

Are States Better at Protecting Their Citizens' Interests Than the Federal Government?

The Marijuana Legalization Process Demonstrates the Interplay Between State and Federal Legislation

Al Krulick

Al Krulick is an award-winning journalist who writes for Debt.org.

Now that residents of Colorado and Washington voted to legalize and regulate the sale of recreational marijuana for adults over 21, and 18 states and the District of Columbia all sanction the legal distribution of medical marijuana, pot advocates believe a tipping point is at hand in the country's relationship with the demon weed.

For years, pot proponents made the moral and ethical arguments that prohibition of any substance, including marijuana, is both an infringement of personal freedom and a misguided policy that helps create a violent, black market sub-culture — much like the prohibition of alcohol did in the last century.

They also challenged the long-term effectiveness of the War on Drugs, pointing out that it has had little success in reducing, much less eradicating, pot usage.

Now these challengers are adding nuance. In an attempt to sway public opinion to their side, more and more anti-drug war warriors point to the economic benefits of making pot legal.

Marijuana by the Numbers

According to federal statistics, about 94 million Americans have tried cannabis at some point in their lives. That's 40 percent of the U.S. population age 12 or older.

Estimates suggest that about 25 million Americans are active pot smokers, consuming some 31 million pounds of marijuana a year.

"The Economics of Marijuana Legalization," by Al Krulick, Debt.org, January 9, 2013. Reprinted by permission.

Yet, according to the U.S. Department of Justice's Bureau of Justice Statistics, American taxpayers spend more than $1 billion a year incarcerating citizens for using pot: nearly one out of every eight drug prisoners in the country is locked up for skirting marijuana laws.

In 2010 alone, more than 850,000 people were arrested for marijuana-related offenses – and most charges were for simple possession.

Jon Gettman's 2007 study "Lost Taxes and Other Costs of Marijuana Laws" found that the U.S. marijuana industry is a $113 billion annual business that costs taxpayers $31.1 billion in lost tax revenues. Gettman, who has a Ph.D. in public policy from George Mason University, suggests that $10.7 billion could be saved each year from the country's $193 billion in annual criminal justice expenditures if marijuana arrests – 5.54 percent of all criminal apprehensions – were stopped.

Last spring, more than 300 economists, including three Nobel Laureates, signed a petition supporting a paper by Harvard economist Jeffrey Miron, who argued the government could save $7.7 billion a year by not having to enforce marijuana prohibition. The report also found that taxing pot at rates comparable to those levied on tobacco and alcohol could raise $6.2 billion annually. That's a total of $13.9 billion in savings and income.

Economist Stephen Easton penned an article in *Businessweek* that suggested the financial benefits of pot legalization may be even bigger than what Miron predicted. Eatson guesses that legalizing the drug could bring in $45 to $100 billion a year.

Taxing Medical Marijuana Brings in Cash

Although the above numbers are all speculative and admittedly somewhat disparate, there are some actual, hard figures reported by states and cities that have had medical marijuana laws in effect for some years. In 2011:

- The city of Oakland, Calif., collected $1.4 million in taxes from medical marijuana dispensaries – nearly 3 percent of all business tax revenue.

- The state of Colorado collected $5 million in sales taxes from the medical marijuana business.
- Denver collected $3.4 million from sales tax, application and license fees for its medical marijuana dispensaries (of which the city has more of than it has Starbucks coffee shops).
- Colorado Springs, Colo., collected more than $700,000 in taxes from the marijuana industry.
- Oregon raised an estimated $6.7 million in taxes which it used to pay for other state health programs.

In 1996, California became one of the first states to legalize medical marijuana. It is estimated that between $700 million and $1.3 billion worth of medical pot is being sold yearly, bringing the state sales taxes of between $58 million and $105 million.

While California voters rejected the most recent attempt to legalize recreational marijuana, the state's tax collectors estimated that legalization would have brought in about another $1.3 billion in needed revenue. Pot is California's biggest cash crop today, ringing up an estimated $14 billion in — except for sanctioned medical marijuana — illegal sales.

It's Always the Economy (Stupid)

It's still too early to gauge the economic effect that legalized marijuana will have on the coffers of the two states that have voted to allow it, but the future looks promising. Estimates for Washington: $2 billion in tax revenue will be raised over the next five years; for Colorado: $600 million in taxes and savings over the same time period.

With numbers like that, pot proponents likely will not have to make the philosophical, moral or legal arguments much longer to win their debate. All they will have to do is point to the balance sheet.

Restoring Balance to State-Federal Relations

Thomas Atwood

Thomas C. Atwood currently serves as Vice President of Institutional Advancement for The Institute of World Politics.

> "When all government, domestic and foreign, in little as in great things, shall be drawn to Washington as the center of all power, it will render powerless the checks provided of one government on another, and will become as venal and oppressive as the government from which we separated."
>
> — Thomas Jefferson

Throughout much of American history, especially since the New Deal, the federal government increasingly has encroached upon the fiscal and constitutional prerogatives of state and local governments. Today, this imbalance has reached a crisis point, and the states are fighting back. Through a variety of initiatives, they are demanding that federal mandates be funded and, in many cases, even are challenging the authority of the federal government to impose these mandates, whether funded or not. With the new, more state-friendly Congress, states and localities have an historic opportunity not only to effect mandate relief, but also to restore balance in state-federal relations.

At one time states and localities saw compliance with Washington's conditions as a small price to pay for federal funding of popular state-implemented programs. But now the federal share of that funding is decreasing while the mandates are becoming more numerous, complex, and expensive. Unfunded federal mandates and highly prescriptive federal programs have backed many states and localities into a fiscal corner, forcing them to sacrifice their own programs and priorities in order to comply with standards set by a distant federal government. Aurora,

"Home Rule: How States Are Fighting Unfunded Federal Mandates," by Thomas Atwood, The Heritage Foundation, December 28, 1994. Reprinted by permission.

Colorado, for example, calculates that it will have to repair some 28,000 curbs in order to comply with the 1990 Americans with Disabilities Act (ADA) at an average cost of $1,500 per curb. Like many municipalities, Aurora simply cannot afford the federal mandate, and the January 1995 deadline for compliance with ADA is looming. Columbus, Ohio's famous 1991 study found that unfunded federal environmental mandates alone will cost their city $856 per household per year by the year 2000. The National Association of State Budget Officers reports that Medicaid's share of state spending will grow from just over 10 percent in 1987 to 20 percent in 1995. Federal Funds Information for States projects state Medicaid spending of $77 billion in 1995. Ohio Governor George Voinovich complained recently of a "forced trade-off between Medicaid and education funding. In the past five years, education declined as a share of state spending... because new Medicaid mandates consume more and more state resources."

Micromanagement by federal agencies imposes costs and one-size-fits-all standards that treat Lubbock like Detroit and Wyoming like New York. For instance, Anchorage, Alaska's sewage inflow was so clean that the municipality could not meet Congress's requirement that all sewage treatment facilities reduce incoming organic waste by at least 30 percent. Still, the federal Environmental Protection Agency insisted that the city meet the arbitrary standard. Anchorage's response was to arrange for two local fisheries to dump fish viscera into the river so the city could remove them. Arizona legislators have complained that the Clean Air Act is too strict even for the naturally occurring dust from Arizona's deserts, let alone automobile emissions. House Majority Leader Brenda Burns commented: "The Clean Air Act's one-size-fits-all standard cannot work in Arizona. We could take every car off the road and still not be in compliance. I suppose we could pave the desert, but I don't think that would be realistic." Federal courts also micromanage the states by mandating state policies ranging from prison library collections to local tax rates to the education of illegal immigrants.

Time and again, Supreme Court decisions have allowed relentless expansion of Congress's enumerated powers.

But states and localities seem to have reached their limit and are fighting back in a number of ways:

- They are publicizing the costs of unfunded federal mandates and holding their Congressmen publicly accountable for mandate votes.
- They are challenging Congress's authority to impose mandates, resisting micromanagement by the federal bureaucracy, and in some instances simply refusing to comply.
- They are suing the federal government for violation of the Tenth Amendment and arguing to constrict the expansive interpretation of the Commerce Clause.
- They are lobbying Congress to pass mandate-relief legislation and to submit for ratification by the states a "no money, no mandate" constitutional amendment.
- They are considering collective action to challenge the federal government's most grievous intrusions on states' autonomy and to amend the Constitution to reaffirm the principles of federalism.

With increasing frequency, these state actions are carried out alongside the efforts of a growing grassroots movement dedicated to reestablishing the constitutional limitations on the federal government. The National Tenth Amendment Committee in Colorado, for example, is working with legislators, activists, and groups in over 40 states to pass resolutions asserting state sovereignty under the Tenth Amendment.

Opposing unfunded federal mandates is a nonpartisan "good government" issue. Whether Republican, Independent, or Democrat, liberal, moderate, or conservative, state and local government officials tend to agree: Washington politicians should not be allowed to take credit for promoting popular causes while states foot the bill. Local officials are quick to add that the same is true of unfunded state mandates. As Newark Mayor Sharpe James states, "If something is important enough to require a state or federal mandate, we should have a voice in deciding how to do it. And if it's important enough to require a mandate, it should be important enough to have state or federal funding to help carry out the mandate."

Prohibiting unfunded federal mandates will restrain overall government spending and regulation and will virtually require Congress to set priorities among programs. It will allow states and localities greater flexibility to devise responses suited to their own particular circumstances, enabling them once again to become "laboratories of democracy." Most important, it will make government more accountable by bringing it closer to the people. Controlling their state legislatures and town councils is far easier than controlling the immense federal bureaucracy.

Counting the Cost

One of the most difficult challenges for states in fighting unfunded federal mandates has been the complexity involved in calculating the costs. The very definition of an "unfunded mandate" is ambiguous. Technically speaking, strings-attached programs, or grants-in-aid, such as Medicaid are not mandates. Theoretically, the state can refuse federal funding and decline to participate in the program. In reality, grants-in-aid are offers the states find it difficult to refuse. To deal with this problem of definition, the Advisory Commission on Intergovernmental Relations (ACIR) has coined the phrase "federally induced costs," a useful umbrella that encompasses all unfunded costs the federal government imposes on states and localities. Generally, when state and local officials complain about unfunded federal mandates, they are thinking of this broader concept.

Even with the problem of definition clarified, the task of calculating the costs of federal mandates is daunting. Hundreds of jurisdictions and agencies can be affected by a single mandate. These entities usually do not have the capacity to monitor the costs. And even if they did, another office would have to assemble the data from all the agencies involved in order to calculate the total. Still, these costs need to be counted, and state and local governments have an interest in making that happen.

Cost Studies

Fortunately, some jurisdictions and research organizations have begun to calculate and publicize the costs of mandates. Among Washington-based state and local government associations, for example, the U.S. Conference of Mayors recently reported that the Clean Water Act alone cost cities with populations greater than 30,000 more than $3.6 billion in 1993. From 1994 through 1998, the ten studied mandates will cost cities $54 billion: the Clean Water Act alone will cost $29.3 billion; the Safe Drinking Water Act, $8.6 billion; and the Resource Conservation and Recovery Act, $5.5 billion. The 1993 survey performed by Price Waterhouse for the National Association of Counties estimated that "counties are spending $4.8 billion annually to comply with just twelve of the many unfunded mandates in federal programs" and that they will spend close to $33.7 billion over the next five years. The National Conference of State Legislatures' regularly updated Hall of States Mandate Monitor tracks Congress's unfunded mandates and mandate-relief legislation.

In 1993, the governments of Tennessee and Ohio issued federal mandate cost studies — the first such studies to be focused on individual states. The Ohio report found that unfunded mandates would cost the state $356 million in 1994 and over $1.74 billion from 1992-1995. Tennessee found that the annual costs of federal mandates imposed between FY 1986-1987 and the end of 1992 would grow from $12 million the first year to $195 million in 1994-1995 and $242 million in 2001-2002. In 1994, Texas reported that its federally induced costs rose from $6.5 billion in the 1990-1991 biennium to $8.9 billion in the 1992-1993 biennium, and $11.4 billion in the 1994-1995 biennium. Among state-based research institutes studying mandate costs are the Wisconsin Policy

Research Institute and the Barry Goldwater Institute for Public Policy Research in Arizona.

Cost figures such as these demonstrate the major impact unfunded federal mandates have on state and local budgets. Union County, North Carolina, cleverly shows the effects of mandates on its budget by itemizing the costs of unfunded state and federal mandates in its tax bills. Moreover, by providing reliable mandate cost figures to the Congressional Budget Office and the Office of Management and Budget, states can help improve the accuracy of these offices' calculations. If states and localities do not develop their own hard numbers, they have less standing to challenge CBO and OMB estimates.

Mandates Auditor Acts

Another way states and localities have begun to address the problem of producing cost figures is by creating mandates auditor offices. In May 1994, Missouri became the first state to establish an office for the sole purpose of tracking federally induced costs. The Missouri legislation charged the "Federal Mandate Auditor" with creating an "inventory of all unfunded federal mandates on all levels of government in the state, calculating by program and agency the cost of such mandates, and performing an historical analysis of year-to-year trends in unfunded federal mandates."

Michigan State Representative Michael Nye plans to introduce a similar bill in 1995 proposing a state "Mandate Ombudsman" and a mandate database. Modeled after a 1993 Mackinac Center for Public Policy proposal, the ombudsman would "track, forecast, disseminate, and distribute information regarding mandated legislation." This new office will coordinate a systematic effort across all agencies of state government to monitor and report on Michigan's federally induced costs.

Publicizing the Problem

State and local officials have developed several creative ways to publicize the problem and hold federal lawmakers accountable to their constituents. Among them:

Mandate-Relief and Tenth Amendment Resolutions

In the past year at least twelve states passed resolutions calling on Congress to pass specific mandate-relief legislation, to fully fund mandates, to stop imposing mandates, and/or to provide cost estimates for any bills that would impose new mandates. But while some state and local officials are satisfied simply to have federal mandates funded, others believe that many mandates represent an overreaching of the federal government's constitutional authority. Eight states (Arizona, California, Colorado, Hawaii, Illinois, Missouri, Oklahoma, and Pennsylvania) expressed this concern in 1994 by passing resolutions that assert state sovereignty under the Tenth Amendment. California's is typical: "The State of California hereby claims sovereignty under the 10th Amendment to the Constitution of the United States over all powers not otherwise enumerated and granted to the federal government by the United States Constitution and that this measure shall serve as notice and demand to the federal government to cease and desist, effective immediately, mandates that are beyond the scope of its constitutionally delegated powers." Some Tenth Amendment resolutions argue further that the states authorized the federal government, not vice versa. According to the National Tenth Amendment Committee, legislators in over twenty states plan to introduce similar resolutions next session. While mandate-relief and Tenth Amendment resolutions may have little or no legal force, they effectively publicize the problem and deliver a clear message to Congress.

Congressional Delegation Mandates Consultation Acts

One particularly effective way states are publicizing the mandate problem is by passing "congressional delegation mandates consultation acts." Noting the recent explosion in federal mandates and the consequent strain on state budgets, these acts "invite" the state congressional delegation to appear before a special session of the legislature to discuss the problem of unfunded federal mandates. Initially, the idea was to invite the state's U.S. Senators, not its entire congressional delegation, to explain their votes on mandate legislation. The theory was that while the Seventeenth Amendment changed the election of senators from election by state legislatures to direct election by the people, it did not change the legal principle of the relationship between U.S. Senators and their respective states. However, all the mandates consultation acts actually introduced invite the entire congressional delegation and the American Legislative Exchange Council's model legislation also invites the entire delegation.

Mandates consultation acts have been passed in seven states. Alabama led the way, adopting the innovative resolution in 1992 under the leadership of State Representative Perry Hooper. South Dakota followed in January 1993. Since then, Arizona, California, Delaware, Michigan, and Pennsylvania have adopted the act.

Alabama, South Dakota, Delaware, and Arizona have held, or attempted to hold, meetings with their congressional delegations. The other three states are scheduling meetings or have not yet followed up on the resolution. In Alabama all nine congressmen participated in the meetings, and all nine signed on to the most far-reaching mandate-relief bills in the 103rd Congress. Despite their participation in meetings, only one of the three in South Dakota's delegation supported a strong mandate-relief measure in 1994. Delaware tried unsuccessfully to schedule meetings, but two out of three from its delegation still supported substantial mandate-relief legislation in 1994. Six out of eight from Arizona's congressional delegation participated in a November 1994 meeting with the state legislature's Committee on Federal Mandates. All six promised to end unfunded federal mandates on states. Concerned about meddlesome federal judges, Senator-elect Jon Kyl (R-AZ) suggested in particular that "it may be time to invoke a little-used portion of the Constitution [Article III, Section 2] that allows the House and Senate to set the parameters of federal judicial powers."

While state legislatures may not have the legal power to require the presence of federal legislators, a Member of Congress who declines the invitation opens himself up to charges of "inside-the-Beltway arrogance." If he accepts, he is not likely to argue for requiring his home state to pay for Washington's latest schemes. More likely, he will profess his faithful opposition to mandates on behalf of his beleaguered state. In any case, he is likely to think twice before voting for the next proposed unfunded mandate he encounters.

Congressional Delegation Voting Reports

Another way to give states leverage over their congressional delegations is to conduct regular voting reports. In 1994, the Virginia House of Delegates expanded the duties of the Commonwealth's liaison office in Washington, D.C., to include "[r]eporting in a timely manner to the General Assembly all federal mandates and regulations which may have an effect on the Commonwealth." The reports are to include "the names of those Virginia congressional members who voted for such mandates and regulations."

In a similar effort to restore accountability, the Arizona-based Barry Goldwater Institute for Public Policy Research has developed a "mandate scorecard" for the U.S. Congress. The November 1994 report scores members of the 103rd Congress for their votes on selected unfunded federal mandates and mandate-relief legislation. Those who voted with the states at least 75 percent of the time are termed "friends of the states," while those who voted with the states less than 25 percent of the time are labeled "foes of the states." Those who scored between 25 percent and 75 percent are labeled "neutral." According to the report, the highest-scoring "friends of the states" were Senators Hank Brown (R-CO), Larry Craig (R-ID), Judd Gregg (R-NH), Dirk Kempthorne (R-ID), Richard Lugar (R-IN), and Alan Simpson (R-WY) and Representatives Chris Cox (R-CA), Jennifer Dunn (R-WA), Thomas Ewing (R-IL), Tillie Fowler (R-FL), Porter Goss (R-FL), Joel Hefley (R-CO), David Levy (R-NY), Howard (Buck) McKeon (R-CA), Dan Miller (R-FL), Dana Rohrabacher (R-CA), Edward Royce (R-CA), and Bob Stump (R-AZ). The lowest scoring "foes of the states" were Senators Max Baucus (D-MT), Barbara Boxer (D-CA), Wendell Ford (D-KY), Howard Metzenbaum (D-OH), Donald Riegle (D-MI), and Paul Wellstone (D-MN) and Representatives John Dingell (D-MI), Sam Gejdenson (D-CT), Barbara Kennelly (D-CT), Jim McDermott (D-WA), Joe Moakley (D-MA), Ray Thornton (D-AR), Craig Washington (D-TX), and Maxine Waters (D-CA).

Mandate voting reports provide a political tool for holding federal lawmakers publicly accountable for shrinking the share of state budgets available for local priorities such as education or police. As these reports become more sophisticated, it may become possible to calculate each senator's or representative's cost to state and local budgets.

Making the Federal Government Pay

The most conspicuous objective of the anti-mandates movement is to require the federal government to fund its mandates on states and localities. State and local officials have considered two approaches: supporting federal mandate-relief legislation and intercepting federal taxes.

Federal Legislation

The "Big Seven" national associations of state and local governments — National Governors' Association, National Conference of State Legislatures, U.S. Conference of Mayors, National Association of Counties, National League of Cities, Council of State Governments, and International City/County Management

Association — have been lobbying Congress resolutely to pass effective mandate-relief legislation.

The Community Regulatory Relief Act (S.993) introduced by Senator Dirk Kempthorne (R-ID) and the Federal Mandate Relief Act of 1993 (H.R.140) sponsored by Representative Gary Condit (D-CA) were strong bills that received widespread attention and support in 1994. Neither addressed existing mandates, but both would have required Congress to fund any new mandates imposed on state and local governments. Both bills had a majority signed on as cosponsors, but neither house's leadership allowed a vote. Congress also failed to vote on less restrictive bills negotiated by Senator Kempthorne and Senator John Glenn (D-OH) and by Representatives John Conyers (D-MI) and William Clinger (R-PA) (H.R. 5128). These bipartisan bills would have established a point of order requiring Congress to authorize funding of mandates whose estimated costs exceed $50 million annually, unless the majority by roll call vote waive the point of order. The bills also would have required CBO cost estimates of private sector mandates exceeding $200 million and executive branch consultations with state and local officials before writing federal regulations.

Shortly after the election, incoming Senate Majority Leader Bob Dole (R-KS) promised Republican governors that "the first bill in the Senate, S. 1., is going to be unfunded mandates." The 104th Congress's mandate-relief agenda will likely build upon and strengthen 1994's bipartisan bills — perhaps by requiring a three-fifths supermajority to waive the point of order; by lowering the $50 million point-of-order threshold; by requiring the appropriation, not just the authorization, of funding for mandates in order to avoid the point of order; or by allowing states and localities not to implement mandates for which funds have not been appropriated. Incoming Senate Judiciary Committee Chairman Orrin Hatch of Utah has indicated his intent to propose a "no money, no mandate" amendment to the Constitution. By offering it simultaneously with a Balanced Budget Amendment (BBA), he hopes to ease the concerns of states and localities which fear that a BBA would lead the federal government to balance its budget by imposing still more unfunded mandates on them. Governors strongly prefer that the two amendments be written as one. State and local leaders also are likely to raise with the 104th Congress broader issues many considered it unrealistic to address in 1994 — issues such as repealing or reforming existing unfunded federal mandates, transferring federal programs to states and localities, compelling federal agencies to allow states greater flexibility in implementing federal programs, and restricting federal judges from directing state and local policies.

The Interception of Federal Taxes

One of the most aggressive approaches to fighting unfunded federal mandates is the possible interception of federal taxes as reimbursement for federally induced costs. For instance, South Carolina State Representative Ralph Davenport introduced a bill in 1994 instructing the State Budget and Control Board to devise a plan for intercepting federal individual and corporate income tax payments made by South Carolina residents to compensate the state for the cost of unfunded federal mandates. The idea had considerable support among legislators but failed to make it out of committee. A few states have considered intercepting federal gasoline taxes in response to the burdensome Clean Air Act. In both cases, it is unclear how the state would manage the interception, considering that federal income and gasoline taxes generally are paid directly by individuals and corporations to the federal government.

There is, however, at least one federal tax states could intercept very easily: the federal income taxes of state employees. Such monies are already in the state treasury, and no collection procedure would have to be altered.

[…]

Federal Programs Are Rife with Fraud, and States Should Not be Dragged Into Corruption

Chris Edwards and Tad DeHaven

Chris Edwards is the director of tax policy at the Cato Institute and author of Downsizing the Federal Government. *Tad DeHaven was a budget analyst on federal and state budget issues for the Cato Institute.*

The federal government is a vast money transfer machine. It spends hundreds of billions of taxpayer dollars each year on subsidy programs—from the massive Medicare to hundreds of more obscure programs that most people have never heard of. There are more than 1,800 federal subsidy programs.

With such a huge array of handouts, the federal budget has become victim to large-scale fraud and abuse—that is, people taking government benefits to which they are not entitled. Just about every subsidy program suffers from fraud and abuse, and we illustrate the problems here with discussions of Medicare, Medicaid, housing programs, student aid, and farm subsidies. Losses to federal taxpayers from fraud, abuse, and other types of improper payments are in the ballpark of $100 billion a year or more.

There have been efforts to reduce improper payments, but the abuse of federal programs continues at high levels. We think that federal subsidy programs should be cut because they harm the economy and are unfair to taxpayers. But endemic fraud and abuse provides an additional reason to pursue cuts and terminations to many federal programs.

"Fraud and Abuse in Federal Programs," by Chris Edwards and Tad DeHaven, Downsizing the Federal Government, August 1, 2009. Reprinted by permission.

Medicare and Medicaid

Fraud in the two main federal health programs is huge, imposing costs on taxpayers at least in the tens of billions of dollars each year. As broad-based government programs, the massive size of Medicare and Medicaid makes them very difficult to police. Medicare, for example, processes 1.2 billion claims each year by computer, generally without human eyes checking them for accuracy.

Let's look first at the fraud and abuse problems in Medicare. The Government Accountability Office estimates that there are about $17 billion of improper Medicare payments each year, including fraudulent and erroneous overpayments to health care providers. That figure does not include the huge new prescription drug benefit, which is thought to be highly susceptible to abuse.

Other estimates of improper Medicare payments are higher. Malcolm Sparrow of Harvard University, a top specialist in health care fraud, argues that estimates by federal auditors do not measure all types of fraud. He believes that as much as 20 percent of federal health program budgets are consumed by fraud and abuse, which would be about $85 billion a year for Medicare.

Sparrow says that criminals can rip off federal health care programs simply by carefully filling out and submitting the proper forms, and then the "claims will be paid in full and on time, without a hiccup, by a computer, and with no human involvement at all." He argues that the abuses do not just stem from occasional overbillings by doctors, but involves organized looting of health care programs by criminals.

A perfect example of what Sparrow is talking about was reported by the *Washington Post* in 2008. A high-school dropout with a laptop computer was able to single-handedly cheat Medicare out of $105 million by electronically submitting 140,000 fraudulent claims over four years for equipment and services.

There are many ways that Medicare gets ripped off: "Billing by health care providers for services not rendered, billing for products not delivered, misrepresenting services, unbundling services, billing for medically unnecessary services, duplicate billing, increasing units of service which are subject to a payment rate, falsifying cost reports resulting in increased payment to the health care provider, kickbacks, and on and on." You can read about the different types of fraud on Medicare's website.

One area of rampant fraud is Medicare's medical equipment subsidies. One scam is for doctors to steer patients into buying motorized wheelchairs that they don't really need, but that Medicare pays for. Then the doctors receive kickbacks from wheelchair supply companies or other operatives. A 2008 report by Senate investigators found that 30 percent of medical equipment reimbursements that they examined appeared to be fraudulent.

Another area of fraud is Medicare's home health care benefits. Medicare pays for home visits by health professionals under certain limited conditions, but patients find ways to illegally get around those limits. In addition, criminal gangs have simply looted this program by submitting false claims. The costs of Medicare home health care coverage soared 44 percent over the last five years, and fraud appears to be an important cause of the increase. Auditors have been concerned about fraud in home health care for years, but the problem never seems to get solved.

The bigger Medicare gets, the more fraud there is. The newest subsidy—the $60 billion a year prescription drug benefit—is thought to be particularly susceptible to abuse. A physicians' publication noted that the benefit was "staggeringly complicated and largely incomprehensible to the very population it was intended to help. It's also ripe with opportunities for the dishonest and fraught with traps for the unwary. ... The drug program's very complexity is a source of fraud."

The Medicaid program also has a giant fraud and abuse problem. The GAO puts the cost of improper Medicaid payments at $33 billion, or about 10.5 percent of the program's total spending. But if improper payments are 20 percent of the program's cost, as Malcolm Sparrow thinks might be the case, that would be a $63 billion annual loss to taxpayers.

New York's Medicaid is especially fraud-ridden. The former chief investigator of the state's Medicaid fraud office believes that about 10 percent of the state's Medicaid budget is consumed by pure fraud, while another 20 to 30 percent is consumed by dubious spending that might not cross the line of being outright criminal.

A 2005 investigation by the *New York Times* found remarkably brazen examples of fraud and abuse in New York's Medicaid. The article noted that the program has "become so huge, so complex, and so lightly policed that it is easily exploited … the program has been misspending billions of dollars annually because of fraud, waste, and profiteering." Here are some of the findings:

- A dentist stole more than $1 million from New York's Medicaid by making claims for fictitious patients and procedures. She even had the chutzpah to make claims for 991 procedures supposedly performed in a single day.
- Medicaid's subsidies for handicapped transportation are widely abused. The program pays $50 per trip for handicapped persons to go to doctor's appointments, but investigators found that many people using the service were not handicapped and that many transportation companies were rigging the system to earn unjustified profits.
- Schools across the state charged Medicaid more than $1 billion for unneeded or unprovided special education activities as a way to bilk the state out of additional Medicaid grant money.
- Criminal gangs diverted Medicaid-covered muscle-building drugs that were intended for AIDS patients to bodybuilders.

Similar schemes to bilk federal health programs are routinely uncovered across the nation. Federal investigators say that they play "whack-a-mole" with organized criminals, because when they crack down on them in one area of the country, they move to a different area and continue bilking federal health programs.

A classic type of fraud in both Medicare and Medicaid is double-billing. In one recent case, the University of Medicine and Dentistry of New Jersey double-billed Medicaid repeatedly over the years by directly submitting claims for outpatient physician services, even as doctors working in the hospital's outpatient centers were submitting their own claims for exactly the same procedures.

Another area of fraud is Medicaid's long-term care benefits, which cover the costs of nursing homes and home care for the elderly poor. Medicaid pays about half of the costs of all long-term care in the nation. The program has complex rules for eligibility related to one's income and financial assets. But nursing homes are expensive, and so the program creates incentives for middle- and higher-income families to try and qualify for it. Indeed, an industry of financial consultants helps seniors hide their income and assets so that they become eligible. This sort of abuse costs taxpayers about one-fifth of the program's cost, or about $13 billion in 2009.

One reason why Medicaid has high levels of fraud is that it is an open-ended "matching" program. The states administer the program and decide how much to spend, but the federal government pays more than half of the costs. That creates a disincentive for state officials to worry too much about fraud and abuse. Indeed, state governments themselves have a history of abusing Medicaid by creating schemes to improperly boost their receipt of federal matching dollars. The *Washington Post* rightly called these state schemes a "swindle," but noted the political resistance to doing anything about it. One solution to these problems is to turn Medicaid into a block grant and freeze the amount of aid to each state. That would immediately give states a big incentive to cut all types of waste, fraud, and abuse.

In sum, the magnitude and complexity of federal health programs results in a huge and ongoing waste of taxpayer funds. Sparrow argues that health care fraud and abuse "might be as low as one hundred billion. More likely two or three. Possibly four or five" hundred billion. The Inspector General of the Department of Health and Human Service told Congress in 2009: "Although it is not possible to measure precisely the extent of fraud in Medicare and Medicaid, everywhere it looks the Office of Inspector General continues to find fraud against these programs."

Housing Subsidies

Federal housing programs have long been a ripe target for fraud and abuse. In 1971, *Time* discussed a scandal at the Federal Housing Administration in which "real estate speculators used the program to make huge profits at the expense of the poor through what amounts to sheer fraud." The article also discussed a scandal from the 1950s whereby "builders pocketed millions of dollars of unearned profit from mortgage loans that exceeded the cost of construction" under a federal program. The magazine concluded that "whenever the government writes a blank check to the housing industry, some sort of scandal is likely to result."

In the 1980s, huge scandals broke out at the Department of Housing and Urban Development involving influence-peddling and gross mismanagement, costing taxpayers billions of dollars. Senior HUD staff were using their positions for personal gain, and when they left HUD they used their inside contacts to win subsidies and contracts. HUD Secretary Sam Pierce favored friends and political allies with contracts, and his mismanagement allowed HUD programs to become targets for abuse by financial and real estate interests.

Today, HUD provides a huge range of subsidies to state and local governments, real estate businesses, financial institutions, and nonprofit groups. The largest share of HUD's budget goes toward rental subsidies for low-income tenants. There are about $1 billion in erroneous and fraudulent overpayments of these subsidies each year, according to the GAO. Tenants make false claims to gain eligibility for rental subsidies, and local public housing authorities (PHAs) have often abused these federal monies.

Public housing is another area of abuse. HUD provides about $8 billion a year to more than 2,000 PHAs. PHAs are infamous for their mismanagement, corruption, and wasteful spending.

HUD is supposed to oversee the PHAs, but its efforts leave a lot to be desired. The *Miami Herald* won a Pulitzer Prize in 2006 for its series exposing fraud and corruption in Miami-Dade›s PHA—a

PHA that had passed HUD audits. Here are some of the abuses uncovered by the *Herald*:

- The PHA gave developers and nonprofit groups with political connections millions of dollars to build affordable housing, but they ended up building shoddy houses or no houses at all.
- HUD gave the PHA $35 million to tear down dilapidated public housing and replace it with new affordable housing. Six years later, half the money was gone, and only three houses had been built. The agency frittered away its money on staff salaries and consultants.
- Instead of selling new houses to low-income buyers, the PHA allowed developers to make sales to wealthy investors who then "flipped" them for a profit.

The Miami-Dade problems are far from unique. For decades, PHAs across the nation have been mishandling taxpayer money. Unfortunately, HUD rarely cuts off the mismanaged PHAs. A *USA Today* article counted 61 PHAs that received funding from the 2009 federal stimulus bill despite repeated financial mismanagement.

Another area of ongoing abuse is the Federal Housing Administration's mortgage loan insurance system. Buyers abuse the system by obtaining loans under false pretenses, and lenders abuse the system by issuing loans for more than properties are worth. These sorts of fraud increase the risks of default, which ultimately costs the taxpayers. As an example, a New Jersey underwriter routinely falsified employment verification documents to obtain FHA-insured mortgages for unqualified borrowers, which resulted in $10 million in losses after 66 mortgages defaulted in 2007.

In sum, programs for public housing, rental assistance, and housing finance have been magnets for fraud and abuse for decades. The Department of Housing and Urban Development ought to be dismantled, and its poor record on controlling fraud and abuse is one good reason why.

Student Loans

Federal student-aid programs have long been subject to fraud and abuse. The three main culprits are students and their families, educational institutions, and lending companies. It is difficult to stop the cheating in student loan programs because they "are large, complex, and inherently risky," according to the Inspector General of the Department of Education. Federal student loan programs involve more than 6,000 postsecondary institutions and more than 3,000 lenders.

Students and their families cheat aid programs by falsely reporting their income level and other items in order to garner larger benefits. With the Pell college grant program, for example, this type of fraud costs taxpayers hundreds of millions of dollars per year. Another abuse is that many students simply decide not to pay back their federal student loans. In 2001, the GAO found that there were more than $20 billion of student loans in default.

Educational institutions often pilfer money meant for students. Under most student loan and grant programs, federal aid is sent to thousands of educational institutions, which are supposed to distribute it to eligible students. However, that distribution system has attracted swarms of shady schools and administrators over the decades that pocket the federal money at the expense of students and taxpayers.

A string of scandals in the early 1990s made clear the magnitude of the problem. One scandal regarded the trade school American Career Training Corporation in Florida. The school recruited new "students" at housing projects and helped them take out loans. The school owners received tens of millions of dollars in federally guaranteed student loans, and simply pocketed it. Another scheme involved 21 Jewish schools in New York State that used millions of dollars in Pell grants to line their pockets while spending little on education. Yet another scandal at the time involved owners of Advanced Business College in Puerto Rico, who used Pell grants to buy $3 million worth of sports cars and real estate for themselves.

A Senate investigation in 1991 found that student loan programs were "plagued with fraud and abuse at every level," which cost taxpayers billions of dollars. The investigation accused the Department of Education of "gross mismanagement, ineptitude, and neglect," finding that it had a "dismal record" of combating loan abuses. Losses from the student loan program totaled an enormous $13 billion between 1983 and 1990. In 1994, the department admitted that it was losing a staggering $3 billion or more annually to waste, fraud, and loan defaults. Education Secretary Richard Riley called the department's oversight "worse than lax."

Today, fraud and abuse may have been reduced from the extraordinarily high levels of the 1980s and 1990s, but there are still large amounts of waste. In 2002, a GAO investigation revealed how easy it was to scam the student loan programs by simply sending in applications under fake student names. In 2005, an investigation found that owners of a company called the CSC Institute stole $4.3 million of the $13 million it received in Pell grants. The GAO currently estimates that taxpayers lose more than $1 billion a year to fraud and abuse in student aid programs.

A new scandal involving financial institutions garnering excessively high profits from student loans has rocked the student-aid industry in recent years. Under the Federal Family Education Loan Program, dozens of loan originators figured out how to earn a 9.5 percent guaranteed return from the government, even though market interest rates have been much lower. Lenders have been able to earn billions of dollars at taxpayer expense. In response, some policymakers argue that private lenders should be cut out of the federal student loan process, and that all lending ought to flow directly from the Department of Education. But the department has been a terrible financial manager of its aid programs, including its direct-loan programs. Thus, the best reform would be to completely terminate the federal role in student aid, and leave the activity to market-based private lending and to charitable organizations.

In 2007, Secretary of Education, Margaret Spellings, testified to Congress that "federal student aid is crying out for reform. The system is redundant, it's Byzantine, and it's broken. In fact, it's often more difficult for students to get aid than it is for bad actors to game the system." She's right, but the system should be ended, not reformed.

Farm Subsidies

The U.S. Department of Agriculture distributes more than $15 billion in cash subsidies to farmers and owners of farmland each year. More than 800,000 farmers and landowners receive subsidies each year, but the payments are heavily tilted toward the largest producers. Indeed, the largest 10 percent of recipients typically receive about 72 percent of all subsidy payments. In 2007, the average income of farm households was $86,223, or 28 percent higher than the average of all U.S. households.

The biggest scandal with farm subsidies is that they exist at all, as discussed elsewhere. But fraud and abuse in farm programs add insult to injury for taxpayers. One GAO study found that improper or fraudulent farm-subsidy payments are as much as half a billion dollars a year. But other GAO studies make clear that the USDA doesn't have a good handle on how much cheating is actually going on. For example, the USDA does not adequately police the income eligibility limits on subsidy programs.

Fraud and abuse in the farm programs takes many forms. Congress puts limits on subsidy payments to particular farmers, but farmers create complex business structures to get around those limits. Farmers are supposed to pay back loans, but farm loan programs have high delinquency rates.

Sloppy administration by the USDA makes cheating easier. A 2007 GAO report found that the USDA paid $1.1 billion in subsidies over six years to 170,000 deceased individuals. There is also the problem of "emergency" farm payments being handed out willy-nilly. After adverse events such as droughts, Congress often dishes out emergency payments to farmers who don't need them or who have not even asked for them. In addition, some farmers will claim to have experienced crop damage even when they haven't in order to receive subsidy payments.

The government response to a drought in 2003 illustrates how emergency subsidies get wasted. Ranchers needed feed for their cattle because of a drought, and the government responded by providing some of its large stockpile of powdered milk. However, much of the free milk ended up being illegally diverted to other uses, which allowed speculators to earn large profits at taxpayer expense.

Finally, the federal crop insurance system operates in a manner that enriches private insurance companies at the expense of taxpayers. The companies receive federal subsidies for providing farm insurance, but those subsidies are not passed through to farmers in the form of lower premiums. Instead, the companies operate like a cartel and are able to earn high profits from excessive premiums, all at taxpayer expense.

Other Federal Programs

Many other federal programs suffer from substantial fraud and abuse. The data cited in the following bullets are from a 2009 GAO report on improper payments, unless otherwise noted:

- Food Stamps. This welfare program is a target for fraud because it is so large and complex. The government must keep track of millions of individuals to accurately document their eligibility while keeping tabs on the 160,000 retailers who deal in food stamps to look for illegal trafficking. In the past, the program spawned a huge black market as recipients exchanged their food stamps for cash on the street. Today, food stamps are issued on electronic cards, and fraud levels have been reduced. Nonetheless, the program's improper payment rate is still about 6 percent, costing taxpayers about $1.7 billion annually.
- School Lunches. A large share of subsidized school meals are taken by families with incomes above the legal cutoff points. Program audits and statistical data have found that about one-quarter of those receiving free and reduced-cost lunches are not eligible. Those unjustified benefits cost taxpayers about $1.4 billion annually.

- Supplemental Security Income. This program pays out $4.6 billion in improper and fraudulent benefits annually.
- Children's Health Insurance Program. About 15 percent, or more than $800 million annually, of CHIP benefits are improper or fraudulent.
- Child Care programs. The federal child care, foster care, and Head Start programs pay out about $900 million in improper and fraudulent benefits annually.
- Temporary Assistance for Needy Families. This program pays out $1.7 billion annually in improper and fraudulent benefits.
- Unemployment Insurance. Almost $4 billion of annual UI benefits are improper or fraudulent.
- Universal Service Fund. This Federal Communications Commission program pays out almost $1.3 billion annually in improper and fraudulent subsidies.
- Earned Income Tax Credit. Almost one-third of EITC payments—$12 billion annually—are improper or fraudulent.
- Veterans Affairs. This department loses at least $800 million annually on improper and fraudulent payments, but the total is likely higher because losses are not reported for all of the department's programs.
- Emergency Response. Subsidies provided in the wake of emergencies are highly susceptible to fraud and abuse because funds are usually pushed out the door quickly with little planning or oversight. Federal recovery aid after Hurricanes Katrina and Rita in 2005 were subject to high levels of waste. The GAO estimated that about $1 billion of payments by the Federal Emergency Management Agency made in just the first sixth months after the storms were "improper and potentially fraudulent."
- Procurement. We have focused on fraud and abuse in federal subsidy programs. But another area of fraud and abuse is federal contracting. Most people have heard of this problem in defense procurement—weapons contractors that rip off federal taxpayers with inflated billings. But fraud and abuse

in contracting are government-wide problems, which hamper
the ability of government programs to operate efficiently.

Conclusions

All kinds of people are using the federal budget as a cookie jar
to garner benefits to which they are not entitled. Families seek
improper benefits through subsidies such as the school lunch
program. Hospitals rip off taxpayers by double billing Medicare and
Medicaid. Criminals loot subsidy programs such as food stamps.
Owners of nonprofit groups that are supposed to aid the needy
line their own pockets with taxpayer funds.

There have been many efforts to end such abuses, but federal
programs are hugely complex and they deliver benefits to thousands
or millions of recipients. Federal agencies are often sloppy in
their administration of programs, and Congress provides little
serious oversight.

Fraud and abuse generate a catch-22 for policymakers who
support spending programs. On the one hand, fraud is clearly
a waste of money and should be stopped. On the other hand,
minimizing fraud requires extensive bureaucratic rules and heavy
enforcement, which reduces program efficiency. In a recent article
on defense procurement, the *Washington Post* noted that reforms
a decade ago intended to make the system more efficient and
entrepreneurial have created the serious side-effect of increasing
various forms of abuse.

A further problem is that Congress has little political incentive
to cut down on waste and abuse. That's because *costs are benefits to
politicians.* If investigators find abuse by, say, a defense contractor
in a member's congressional district, that member will usually
be inclined to take the contractor's view of things. After all, if the
contractor overbilled federal taxpayers, it just means that more
money was spent in the member's district. Of course, members
of Congress must look as if they are on the side of the taxpayer,
and so they will hold occasional oversight hearings to investigate

abuses. But sustained congressional efforts to really combat waste, fraud, and abuse in the federal budget are rare.

In sum, fraud and abuse is a serious shortcoming of many federal programs. It is appalling that $100 billion a year—or perhaps much more—of benefits are misappropriated by people not entitled to them. Federal subsidies for industries such as health care and education ought to be cut because private markets can usually perform these activities better than governments. But the endemic fraud and abuse experienced by many government programs provides an additional reason to pursue major cuts in the federal budget.

The Federal Government Is Better Equipped to Financially Assist Students

Bridget Terry Long

Bridget Terry Long is the Saris Professor of Education and Economics and the former Academic Dean at the Harvard Graduate School of Education.

Higher education plays an important role in U.S. society. In addition to providing numerous public benefits, such as an increased tax base and greater civic engagement, it helps individuals attain economic and social success. Experiences and skills acquired from postsecondary education reverberate throughout life in terms of higher earnings, a lower likelihood of unemployment, and better decisions about health. Yet research demonstrates that one of the primary barriers to college enrollment, especially for low-income students, is the financial outlay required to attend. For this reason, the federal and state governments spent more than $2.5 trillion in 2008-09 on student grants, such as Pell Grants, with the hope of encouraging enrollment.

Although there is a belief that financial aid could greatly improve educational outcomes, there also are many reasons to question the efficacy of the nation's current system of financial aid. After decades of financial aid policy, there are still significant gaps in college access by income, even after accounting for differences in academic preparation and achievement by income. Low-income high school graduates in the top academic quartile attended college at only the same rate as high-income high school graduates in the bottom quartile of achievement. Such gaps, which are also evident in terms of race and ethnicity, suggest that the aid system has not equalized access to higher education. A 2006 review of the

"Making College Affordable by Improving Aid Policy," by Bridget Terry Long, University of Texas at Dallas, 2010. Reprinted by permission.

aid system by the federal Commission on the Future of Higher Education concluded what many observers have voiced for years: The financial aid system is not addressing the problems facing students. Although financial aid can dramatically reduce the overall cost of college, many students still have significant unmet need. Moreover, the receipt of financial aid is predicated on navigating a lengthy, complicated process. As noted by the commission, some students "don't enter college because of inadequate information and rising costs, combined with a confusing financial aid system."

Although the financial aid system is imperfect, years of research support the notion that financial aid can influence students' postsecondary decisions. Research has identified effective financial aid policies that improve college enrollment and choice, and the lessons learned from these studies could help inform current debates about how to improve the financial aid system.

Three main lessons are clear from the numerous studies on financial aid. The first lesson is that information and the design of a policy are crucial factors in determining whether a policy is effective in improving access. Therefore, policies should balance the need to target limited resources at specific groups with the fact that making aid application and award processes too complicated is likely to deter students. Second, while recent years have witnessed the growth of merit-based aid, these programs often favor more affluent students who are likely to attend college regardless of whether they are given financial aid. Therefore, if the goal of the nation's limited financial aid resources is to influence decisions, then there is a strong case to focus on need-based awards. Obviously, grants have larger direct costs than loans, and so loans may be considered a less expensive way to help students. However, the third lesson from the research literature is that loans have their own indirect, long-term costs, which are hard to fully predict or put in monetary terms. Debt can affect educational decisions as well as decisions long after leaving college in ways that are suboptimal to both the individual and society.

The Affordability Problem

Although there are many barriers to college access and success, a major impediment is cost. As the Commission on the Future of Higher Education concluded, "There is no issue that worries the American public more about higher education than the soaring cost of attending college." During the 2009-10 school year, the College Board found that the average total tuition and fees at public four-year colleges and universities was $7,020, with average total charges amounting to $15,213. Without any financial aid, the total cost amounts to 30% of the annual median family income. Concerns about affordability are even greater at private four-year colleges and universities, which charged an average tuition of $26,273, or $35,636 including room and board. This constitutes more than half the annual income of a median family. The average low-income student attends and faces the costs of a local community college, and the average full-time tuition at these institutions was $2,544 in 2009-10.

The current situation is the result of skyrocketing prices during the past several decades. From 1979-80 to 2009-10, the average cost of a public, four-year institution increased from $738 to $7,020, a multiple of three times after accounting for inflation. Meanwhile, the median family income has not nearly kept pace with growing tuition costs. Given the high cost of college relative to family incomes, at least some amount of financial aid is necessary for most families.

Of course, financial aid has been a staple of higher education for several decades. To understand the degree to which the current system meets the financial needs of students, one must calculate the price students pay for college after financial aid. After taking into account the multiple sources of financial assistance, the price paid by students is much lower than the list prices in college catalogues. According to the College Board, in 2009-10, the average net price at a public, four-year college was $9,810 and $21,240 at a private, four-year college. Although net tuition prices are significantly lower on average than list price, it is important to keep in mind that these are only mean values with a great deal of variation across and within institutions. Differences in net price at the same school may be based on differences in financial resources, family makeup, and student characteristics, such as academic ability. In a study of the practices of very selective private colleges and universities, which tend to focus on need-based financial aid, researchers found that the net price students face could vary from $7,495 for students from the lowest quintile of family income to $16,249 for students from families in the upper-middle quintile and $23,399 for students in the highest income quintile.

Although the costs faced by students are much less when grant aid is considered, the remaining costs that families must meet are often substantial. A study I did with Erin Riley in 2007 documented the significant amount of unmet financial need faced by many students, particularly students from low-income backgrounds and students of color. After accounting for the family's expected contribution and the receipt of all grants, dependent students in 2003-04 faced an average unmet need of $7,195. Increasingly, students are turning to loans to make up this remaining difference. However, even after taking into account government and institutional loans, there is still significant unmet need. Researchers have found, for example, that dependent students faced $5,911 in unmet need ($4,503 for older, independent students) after grants and loans.

Although the nation spends billions of dollars each year on financial aid, the estimates on unmet need suggest the current amount of funding may not be enough. Therefore, many calls for reform have focused on increasing the level of financial aid awards. Recent legislation has targeted this problem. With the federal Health Care and Education Reconciliation Act, signed March 30, 2010, the budget for Pell Grants increased more than $40 billion. Still, this is not enough to significantly reduce unmet need for most students, especially with the continually rising costs of higher education. Therefore, reviews of the research literature should keep in mind how inadequate funding levels may limit the effectiveness of current forms of aid. But rather than just asking for more, it is necessary to consider the best ways to alter the aid system guided by what is known about the types of aid and particular policy designs that are most effective.

Does Lowering Costs Increase Enrollment?

Grants, or aid that does not need to be repaid, tend to be the focus of most research on financial aid. Although some programs have not demonstrated a large enrollment effect, others have spurred much greater responses. The nature of grants has also changed in recent years. Although the original intent of most grant programs was to increase college access for students who would not have otherwise been able to attend, governments during the 1990s began to introduce grant programs with a very different focus and design. It is useful, then, to identify the distinguishing characteristics of the most effective polices and consider how the change in the focus of grant programs has affected affordability for different income groups.

Because grants are not given randomly to students, but rather often involve favoring students with need or merit or both, a straightforward comparison of students eligible for grants with those who are not eligible gives only a partial view of the role of financial aid. Such comparisons do not isolate the effects of aid from other differences between students, such as background or academic preparation. In recent years, the best studies have used experimental or "natural experiments" to discern the impact of financial aid. The introduction of a new program that affects some students but not others can provide a useful research opportunity with the aid-eligible students being the "treatment group" and ineligible students being the "control group." In several cases, researchers have compared the enrollment rates of the two groups before and after the creation of a new policy. This type of work has found that subsidies that reduce college prices increase attendance rates, attainment, and choice.

The Pell Grant, which was introduced in 1972 as the Basic Education Opportunity Grant, is the nation's largest need-based grant program. Research on its effectiveness, however, has left more puzzles than answers. In one line of study, researchers have compared the enrollment rates of low-income students before and after 1972, with ineligible students serving as a control group. In a 1996 study, Thomas Kane found that contrary to program expectations, enrollment grew 2.6 percentage points *more slowly* for the lowest income quartile, the expected beneficiaries of the Pell Grant. Other research also found no disproportionate growth in college enrollment or completion of a bachelor's degree by low-income students after the introduction of the Pell Grant. Only public two-year college enrollment seemed to grow more quickly for low-income youth. Interestingly, in other research, the impact of the Pell Grant was found to be large and positive for older students, suggesting that the effects of aid can vary by age.

There are several theories as to why the introduction of the Pell Grant did not result in an increase in the enrollment of traditional-age, low-income students. Some observers suggest that Pell might have had an impact only on college choice, rather than on attendance, as there may have been relative shifts in enrollment among different types of colleges. Others have instead suggested that Pell may have worked well enough to maintain the distribution of students during the 1970s and 1980s; without it, enrollment rates would have fallen much more. However, the most convincing explanations for the lack of a response among low-income students to the Pell Grant focus on problems with the program itself. Researchers suggest that low program visibility, the complexity of the application process, and intimidating audit procedures contributed to limiting the aid program's impact. It is important to note that the current Pell Grant program is somewhat different than it was in the early 1970s. Therefore, it is unclear whether these studies reflect on the present nature and effectiveness of the policy.

A wave of more recent research has done a much better job discerning the effectiveness (or lack thereof) of a variety of federal and state financial aid policies. Using a number of different research approaches, several studies have convincingly established causal estimates of financial aid programs and given much clearer answers about the potential effectiveness of grants.

Susan Dynarski, for example, examined the impact of eliminating the Social Security Student Benefit (SSSB) program, which gave monthly support to children (age 18 to 22) of dead, disabled, or retired Social Security beneficiaries while they were enrolled full-time in college. At its peak, the program provided grants totaling $3.3 billion annually to one out of 10 students. In 1982, Congress decided to discontinue the program. According to one study, this step reduced college access and attainment by a difference of over 25% between the treatment and control groups. This translates into $1,000 (in 1997 dollars) of grant aid increasing education attainment by 0.20 years and the probability of attending college by 5 percentage points. In contrast to the Pell Grant, awareness among potential beneficiaries of the SSSB program was high due to notification from the government and the extremely simple application process. This gives early clues to the importance of policy and program design.

The Georgia HOPE Scholarship is another grant program that has been evaluated. Introduced in 1993, the program pays for the in-state public tuition of Georgia residents with at least a B average in high school; residents choosing to attend in-state private colleges received $3,000 during the early years of the program. Similar to the SSSB, the HOPE Scholarship is simple in design and much effort was made to publicize the program and to train high school guidance counselors on how to help their students access the program. Dynarski compared enrollment rates in Georgia with rates in other southern states before and after the program, and the results showed that Georgia's program has had a surprisingly large impact on the college-attendance rate of middle- and high-income youth. The results suggest that each $1,000 in aid (in 1998 dollars) increased the college attendance rate in Georgia by 3.7 to 4.2 percentage points. Also, there was a much larger impact on college choice. Chris Cornwell and David Mustard also examined Georgia HOPE using a different data set, and they estimated that the scholarship increased the overall freshmen enrollment rate by 6.9 percentage points, with the gains concentrated in four-year schools.

The Cal Grant is another large state grant program. Its eligibility criteria mix both need and merit as students must meet thresholds in income, assets, and high school GPA. The results of a study by Kane have suggested that there are large effects (3 to 4 percentage points) of grant eligibility on college enrollment among financial aid applicants, with larger effects on the choice of private four-year colleges in California. Unlike with the SSSB and Georgia HOPE Scholarship, the large response to the Cal Grant seems to be *in spite of* its design. Some suspect that the impact of the program could have been larger, because reports indicate many eligible students, as many as 19,000, failed to apply.

Implications for Aid Policy

In summary, the research suggests aid programs can be successful as price and financial aid have been found to influence students' decisions about college. The programs that have been the most effective are those that are relatively easy to understand and apply for and that include efforts to ensure that potential beneficiaries are aware of them. This observation begs the question: What do students and their families know about financial aid? In order to have an impact on behavior, students and their families must be aware of the policies designed to help them. Unfortunately, awareness appears to be a major barrier to college access, as many students lack accurate information about higher education costs and financial aid. Researchers have continually found a significant lack of information among prospective college students. Most studies have suggested that students and their parents greatly overestimate the costs of college. There also is a lot of misinformation about financial aid among parents and students. A Harris Poll commissioned by the Sallie Mae Fund found that two-thirds of all parents and all young adults planning to go to college did not name grants as a possible source of funds when asked about types of financial aid. Awareness about aid and college costs appears to be especially limited among low-income students.

The low levels of awareness about aid and the misinformation of many families has serious implications for the effectiveness of any policy or program. In a world with many misinformed or unaware families, unless a program is highly publicized and simple to access, it is unlikely to have a major impact on college enrollment. Implicit in policy design are tradeoffs between making a program simple to understand and the need to limit eligibility to only a subset of students due to finite resources. On the one hand, in order to have an impact on behavior, students and their families must be aware of the policies designed to help them and understand how to access them. On the other hand, given the focus on helping a particular type of student (e.g., financially needy students), some type of means testing must be in place to ensure that only students with actual need (or some other criteria) are eligible to receive the aid. For these reasons of efficiency, many arguments have been made for elaborate application procedures for such need-based programs as the Pell Grant. However, introducing complexity into how aid is awarded can also be a source of informational barriers.

Critiques of the Free Application for Federal Student Aid (FAFSA) and the general aid application process highlight the tradeoffs between simplicity and means testing that must be balanced in policy design. At its most basic level, the FAFSA attempts to discern how financially needy students are in order to determine how to distribute limited government financial aid. It collects a wealth of information about a family's situation in the hope of equitably treating families with similar situations. However, many critics surmise that the lack of information about financial aid is linked to this process. A major critique is that the FAFSA is long and cumbersome. Until recently, to determine eligibility, students and their families had to fill out an eight-page, detailed form containing over 100 questions. To answer three of these, students had to complete three additional worksheets with nearly 40 additional questions. Even the lowest income students, who had already established their eligibility for other federal means-tested programs and were known to be eligible for federal student aid, had to go through this arduous process. Not surprisingly, research suggests that students and their families are often confused and even deterred by the form. In a 2004 study, Jacqueline King found that half of the 8 million undergraduates enrolled in 1999-2000 at institutions that participate in the federal student aid program did not complete the FAFSA. Yet 850,000 of them—more than 20%—would have been eligible for a Pell Grant. Furthermore, of those who did file, more than half missed the application deadline to be eligible for additional state and institutional aid programs.

Given this and other critiques of the FAFSA, many people suggest that perhaps the application process leans too far toward complexity without balancing the need to make the process clear and reasonable for students. Recently, calls to simplify the financial aid process have spurred the Department of Education to implement several changes. The FAFSA now uses "skip logic" in its online version to eliminate questions that do not apply to some students and to give students instant estimates of the Pell Grant and student loan eligibility. The department also is piloting ways to transfer information directly from the IRS to the online FAFSA. These efforts still require families to be aware of the FAFSA and to be able to complete it online, preferably with high-speed internet, but they are still steps in the right direction. Moreover, the Department of Education currently is revising the FAFSA4caster tool to more easily give families early estimates of their financial aid eligibility.

Current research projects are also exploring interventions that might deal with concerns about the financial aid application process. For example, working with Eric Bettinger, Philip Oreopoulos, and Lisa Sanbonmatsu, I developed a project in which tax preparers help low-income families complete their FAFSAs. The intervention streamlined the aid application process and students' access to accurate and personalized higher educational information. Using a random assignment research design, H&R Block tax professionals helped a group of eligible low- to middle-income families complete the FAFSA. Then, families were immediately given an estimate of their eligibility for federal and state financial aid as well as information about local postsecondary options. Early project results confirm suspicions that a lack of information and the complexity of the aid process are hindering low- and moderate-income students' ability to apply for aid and enroll in college. We found that individuals who received assistance with the FAFSA and information about aid were substantially more likely to submit the aid application. More importantly, the program also increased college enrollment for the dependent students and for young adults with no prior college experience. Although it will take time to determine the full benefits and costs of simplification, these results suggest that streamlining the application process and providing better information could be effective ways to improve college access. The results also lend additional support to the idea that the most effective aid policies are those in which there are high levels of awareness and the application is relative simple.

Need-Based Versus Merit-Based Aid

While research demonstrates that grants are effective in encouraging college access, it is also worth considering which types of grants have the largest impact on enrollment rates. To answer this question, it is necessary to ask, who needs support in order to attend college? In other words, what kinds of students might be encouraged to attend college with price subsidies? Although affordability, or the comfort level of paying for the expense, is a concern of all students, most middle- and upper-income students will attend college regardless of whether they receive financial aid. In contrast, the problem of college access, defined as whether to attend college at all, is substantial for low-income students, as illustrated by the gaps in college attendance by income and substantial levels of unmet need for this group. Therefore, if the goal is to maximize the impact of a dollar on college enrollment rates, funds should be directed toward this group. Not surprisingly, price and financial aid have often been found to have larger effects on the enrollment decisions of lower- rather than higher-income students.

Based on the above reasoning, it is important to note that the research literature documents that different types of grants vary in who and how they affect college decisions. For instance, the merit-based Georgia HOPE Scholarship had large effects on college access overall, but the benefits of the program were not evenly distributed. Researchers found that the program widened the gap in college attendance between those from low- and high-income families and between black and white students. In sum, the program disproportionally helped upper-income students. Moreover, the major impact of the policy was on college choice rather than enrollment; that is, Georgia HOPE influenced the enrollment choices of students who would have otherwise attended a different college or university. Although choice is an issue worth considering, whether a student attends college at all is a more important concern.

Georgia HOPE marked the beginning of a larger trend toward shifting state aid from a need-based to merit-based focus, as many other state merit-based aid programs have followed. Although more money is allocated by states to need-based programs, according to NASSGAP, after accounting for inflation, spending on non-need based grant aid grew 203% during the past decade, compared with only 60% growth in need-based grant aid. These other state policies have differed in how they define merit, in funding sources, and in the impact they have had on student outcomes. Dynarski found that the degree to which more affluent students are favored in these state aid programs appears to be related to how stringent the merit aid criteria are. In other words, the degree to which merit is used in aid criteria has profound effects on whether the policy influences college access among low-income students rather than choice or affordability for upper-income students. Given that the opportunity to perform well on some of the merit-based criteria is related to income either directly or indirectly through school quality, even high-achieving, low-income students can be at a disadvantage for qualifying for merit-based awards. Some researchers have concluded that even among students of equal academic merit, increased emphasis on merit in financial aid may exacerbate the trend toward greater income inequality.

Recent federal aid policies also have moved away from focusing on increasing the basic access of low-income students. In 1992, federal financial need calculations began to exclude home equity, thereby allowing many more middle-class families to qualify for federal need-based support. That year, the Stafford Unsubsidized Loan Program was also created, which made student loans available to all families regardless of income. Then, in 1997, the federal government introduced the higher education tax credits, which were available to families with incomes up to $100,000, far above the national family income average. Most recently, the creation in 2006 of the Academic Competitiveness Grants introduced merit criteria into federal aid for undergraduates. The program gives Pell Grant recipients additional funds for completing certain courses and maintaining a 3.0 GPA in college.

The shifting of aid priorities from need to other criteria becomes clear when juxtaposing the aforementioned trends to what has happened with need-based aid. Whereas other forms of aid have grown, need-based grants have not kept pace. Since its inception, the Pell Grant has declined substantially in value, compared with tuition prices. According to the College Board, in 2008 dollars, the maximum Pell Grant in 1976-77 was $5,393; it was only $5,800 by 2008-09, even though tuition rates grew exponentially during the same period. Despite the recent action to increase the Pell Grant maximum, with so much lost ground, many low-income students still have significant unmet needs.

There is no question that addressing issues of affordability and rewarding performance with merit-based aid are justified goals. However, as demonstrated by research, shifting aid priorities to other goals has negative repercussions for the important goal of increasing access. Careful attention must be paid to the exact criteria used when awarding aid for fear of duplicating the sometimes unfavorable effects that have been found with other types of grants, such as merit-based aid. Again, the question worth asking is: What is the best use of limited funds in order to increase participation?

[...]

Making Financial Aid Policy More Effective

Given the critical role higher education plays in both individual economic success and the public good, increasing college access should be a major government goal. However, despite substantial increases in access to higher education during the past several decades, postsecondary attendance nationwide continues to be stratified by family income, and students, particularly those with lower incomes, have significant unmet need. In consideration of this problem, it is important to review the evidence on which aid programs have been more effective and why. Aid can work to increase college enrollment, but some programs and formats have been more successful meeting this goal than others. Three lessons can be taken from the extensive research literature on financial aid.

First, when designing an aid program, information and simplicity are important. What is clear from the literature is that the mere existence of an aid program is not enough to encourage enrollment, because the visibility and design of the program also clearly matter. In several cases, researchers have not observed large, general responses to the introduction of financial aid programs (e.g., the Pell Grant). On the other hand, research on examples of highly publicized financial aid programs characterized as being simpler in design and application has found large enrollment responses (e.g., the Social Security Student Benefit Program and the Georgia HOPE Scholarship). In summary, the research suggests aid programs are most successful when they are well publicized and relatively easy to understand and apply for. This conclusion has strong implications for the FAFSA, which needs to be substantially simplified. Moreover, there are calls to enhance the visibility of aid programs, as my research with Bettinger, Oreopoulos, and Sanbonmatsu has shown that such efforts can have dramatic effects on college enrollment rates.

Second, need-based aid is more effective in increasing access for low-income students than other forms of aid. One of the original and most prominent goals of financial aid policy was to enable the college attendance of students who would not otherwise be able to attend. Given gaps in enrollment by income, much of policy has focused on low-income students. However, with the movement from need-based to merit-based and other forms of aid, this aim is being lost. Merit-based aid programs favor more affluent students, and similar results have been found in terms of the federal Higher Education Tax Credits and college savings programs. Given these facts, along with the recognition that the government has limited resources, more attention should be paid to targeting students whose decisions might actually be altered by financial aid, as opposed to helping students who would attend regardless. For low-income students, this means focusing on need-based grants.

Third, all aid is not equal. Grants have been shown to be effective in influencing student decisions if designed properly, whereas loans are less effective in increasing enrollment. Moreover, the increased complexity of loans and their potential negative impact on longer-term outcomes should also be taken into account. Debt burden can have negative effects on a range of outcomes, and it is unclear if recent efforts to reduce the interest rate on government loans and to extend the federal loan forgiveness program will do much to mitigate these indirect effects. Therefore, the government should be cautious in its recent trend toward using loans as the primary form of student financial aid.

The Rights of US Citizens

The Green Party of the United States

The Green Party of the United States is an environmentally conscious political party. It also promotes nonviolence, social justice, participatory, grassroots democracy, gender equality, LGBT rights, anti-war, and anti-racism.

The foundation of any democratic society is the guarantee that each member of society has equal rights. Respect for our constitutionally protected rights is our best defense against discrimination and the abuse of power. Also, we recognize an intimate connection between our rights as individuals and our responsibilities to our neighbors and the planet. The Green Party shall strive to secure universal and effective recognition and observance of the principles and spirit expressed in the United National Universal Declaration of Human Rights as an international standard that all nations must meet.

One of our key values is respect for diversity. We are committed to establishing relationships that honor diversity; that support the self-definition and self-determination of all people; and that consciously confront the barriers of racism, sexism, homophobia, class oppression, ageism, and the many ways our culture separates us from working together. We support affirmative action to remedy discrimination, to protect constitutional rights and to provide equal opportunity under the law.

Women's Rights

Since the beginning of what we call civilization, when men's dominance over women was firmly established, until the present day, our history has been marred with oppression of and brutality to

"Social Justice," The Green Party of the United States. http://www.gp.org/social_justice_2016. Reprinted by permission.

women. The Green Party deplores this system of male domination, known as patriarchy, in all its forms, both subtle and overt — from oppression, inequality, and discrimination to all forms of violence against women and girls including rape, trafficking, forced sex which is also rape, slavery, prostitution and violence against women within marriage and relationships and in all institutions. The change the world is crying for cannot occur unless women's voices are heard. Democracy cannot work without equality for women, which provides equal participation and representation. It took an extraordinary and ongoing fight over 72 years for women to win the right to vote. However, the Equal Rights Amendment, first introduced in 1923, has still not been ratified by 2012, representing a continuous struggle of 87 years with no victory in sight. We believe that equality should be a given, and that all Greens must work toward that end. We are committed to increasing participation of women in politics, government and leadership so they can change laws, make decisions, and create policy solutions that affect and will improve women's lives, and we are building our party so that Greens can be elected to office to do this. In July 2002 the National Women's Caucus of the Green Party of the United States was founded to carry out the Party's commitment to women.

We also support, and call on others to support, the many existing and ongoing efforts for women:

Social Equality
We support the equal application of the Constitution of the United States of America to all citizens, and therefore call for passage of the Equal Rights Amendment (ERA). We urge accelerated ratification by three or more of the remaining 15 states that are required to pass ERA into law and into the Constitution. We urge renewed efforts and campaigns to ratify the ERA. We support the Equal Rights Amendment reintroduced in the U.S. Congress, and support using the precedent of a three-state strategy for ratification.

We call for equal representation of women in Congress instead of the current 17% in 2012.

The Green Party calls for U.S. passage of CEDAW, the Convention on the Elimination of all forms of Discrimination Against Women, which was adopted in 1979 by the U.N. General Assembly and ratified by 173 countries. The U.S. is one of the very few countries, and the only industrialized nation, that have not ratified it.

The Equal Employment Opportunities Commission should actively investigate and prosecute sexual harassment complaints. Women who file complaints must not be persecuted and should be protected under federal and state law. We must enshrine in law the basic principle that women have the same rights as men, and promote gender equality and fairness in the work force to ensure that women receive equal pay for jobs of equal worth.

We support the inclusion of an equal number of women and men in peace talks and negotiations, not only because these efforts directly affect their lives and those of their husbands, children and families, but also because when women are involved, the negotiations are more successful.

Reproductive Rights
Women's rights must be protected and expanded to guarantee each woman's right as a full participant in society, free from sexual harassment, job discrimination or interference in the intensely personal choice about whether to have a child.

Women's right to control their bodies is non-negotiable. It is essential that the option of a safe, legal abortion remains available. The "morning-after" pill must be affordable and easily accessible without a prescription, together with a government-sponsored public relations campaign to educate women about this form of contraception. Clinics must be accessible and must offer advice on contraception and the means for contraception; consultation about abortion and the performance of abortions, and; abortion regardless of age or marital status.

We endorse women's right to use contraception and, when they choose, to have an abortion. This right cannot be limited to women's age or marital status. Contraception and abortion must be included in all health insurance policies in the U.S., and any state government must be able to legally offer these services free of charge to women at the poverty level. Public health agencies operating abroad should be allowed to offer family planning, contraception, and abortion in all countries that ask for those services. We oppose our government's habit of cutting family planning funds when those funds go to agencies in foreign countries that give out contraceptive devices, offer advice on abortion, and perform abortions.

We encourage women and men to prevent unwanted pregnancies. It is the inalienable right and duty of every woman to learn about her body and to be aware of the phases of her menstrual cycle, and it is the duty for every man to be aware of the functions and health of his and his partner's bodies. This information is necessary for self-determination, to make informed decisions, and to prevent unintended consequences. Unplanned conception takes control away from individuals and makes them subject to external controls. The "morning-after" pill and option of a safe and legal abortion need to remain available.

[…]

Rights of the Disabled

We support the full enforcement of the Americans with Disabilities Act to enable all people with disabilities to achieve independence and function at the highest possible level. Government should work to ensure that children with disabilities are provided with the same educational opportunities as those without disabilities.

The physically and mentally challenged are people who are differently abled from the majority, but who are nevertheless able to live independently. The mentally ill are people with serious mental problems who often need social support networks. Physically and mentally challenged people have the right to live independently in their communities. The mentally ill also have the right to live independently, circumscribed only by the limitations of their illness. These people are their own best advocates in securing their rights and for living in the social and economic mainstream.

Current Medicaid policy forces many challenged people to live in costly state-funded institutions. Excluding these people from society alienates them; excluding them from the work force denies them the chance to use their potentials. The diminishing funds available to provide care for the growing number of the mentally ill often result in their homelessness, vagrancy and dependence on short-term crisis facilities. Lack of funding also increases the necessity of placing them in long-term, locked facilities. The Green Party urges the government to:

- Increase rehabilitation funding so that persons with disabilities can pursue education and training to reach their highest potential. The differently abled should participate fully in the allocation decisions of state rehabilitation departments' funds.
- Aggressively implement the Americans with Disabilities Act.
- Fund in-home support services to allow the differently abled to hire personal care attendants while remaining at home.
- Allocate adequate funding to support community-based programs that provide out-patient medical services, case management services and counseling programs. We should provide a residential setting within the community for those who do not need institutional care but who are unable to live independently.
- Make it easier for the chronically mentally ill to apply for and receive Supplemental Security Income.
- Mainstream the differently abled. Increase teacher training in regard to the needs of differently abled students.
- Discourage stereotyping of the mentally and physically challenged by the entertainment industry and the media.
- Fund programs to increase public sensitivity to the needs of the mentally ill and differently abled.

[...]

Organizations to Contact

The editors have compiled the following list of organizations concerned with the issues debated in this book. The descriptions are derived from materials provided by the organizations. All have publications or information available for interested readers. This list was compiled on the date of publication of the present volume; the information provided here may change. Be aware that many organizations take several weeks or longer to respond to inquiries, so allow as much time as possible.

The Council of State Governments (CSG)

CSG National Headquarters
1776 Avenue of the States
Lexington, KY 40511
phone: (859) 244-8000
email: membership@csg.org
website: www.csg.org

The Council of State Governments is the nation's only organization serving all three branches of state government. CSG is a region-based forum that fosters the exchange of insights and ideas to help state officials shape public policy.

National Association of Counties (NACo)

660 North Capitol Street NW
Suite 400
Washington, DC 20001
phone: (888) 407-NACo (6226)
email: research@naco.org
website: www.naco.org/

The National Association of Counties (NACo) unites America's 3,069 county governments. NACo brings county officials together to advocate with a collective voice on national policy and exchange ideas.

National Conference of State Legislatures (NCSL)
444 North Capitol Street, NW, Suite 515
Washington, DC 20001
phone: (202) 624-5400
email: ncslnet-admin@ncsl.org
website: www.ncsl.org/

The National Conference of State Legislatures is committed to the success of all legislators and staff. Their mission is to improve the quality and effectiveness of state legislatures, promote policy innovation and communication, and ensure state legislatures have a strong, cohesive voice in the federal system.

National Governors Organization
444 North Capitol St. NW #267
Washington, DC 20001
phone: (202) 624-5300
email: webmaster@nga.org
website: www.nga.org/cms/home

The National Governors Association—the bipartisan organization of the nation's governors—promotes visionary state leadership, shares best practices, and speaks with a collective voice on national policy.

Organization of American States
17th Street and Constitution Ave., NW
Washington, DC, 20006-4499
phone: (202) 370-5000
website: www.oas.org/en/

The Organization of American States was established in order for its members to achieve "an order of peace and justice, to promote their solidarity, to strengthen their collaboration, and to defend their sovereignty, their territorial integrity, and their independence."

Tenth Amendment Center
PO Box 13458
Los Angeles, CA 90013
phone: (213) 935-0553
email: info@tenthamendmentcenter.com
website: http://tenthamendmentcenter.com/

The Tenth Amendment Center seeks to teach people about the original meaning of the Constitution. They lead powerful grassroots coalitions to use nullification as a means to block federal overreach.

Bibliography

Books

Akhil Reed Amar. *The Constitution Today: Timeless Lessons for the Issues of Our Era*. New York, NY: Basic Books, 2016.

Fergus M. Bordewich. *The First Congress: How James Madison, George Washington, and a Group of Extraordinary Men Invented the Government*. New York, NY: Simon & Schuster, 2016.

Adam Freedman. *A Less Perfect Union: The Case for States' Rights*. New York, NY: Broadside Books, 2015.

Adam Freedman. *The Naked Constitution: What the Founders Said and Why It Still Matters*. New York, NY: Broadside Books, 2012.

Alexander Keyssar. *The Right to Vote: The Contested History of Democracy in the United States*, Revised Edition. New York, NY: Basic Books, 2009.

Michael J. Klarman. *The Framers' Coup: The Making of the United States Constitution*. New York, NY: Oxford University Press, 2016.

David M. Konisky. *Failed Promises: Evaluating the Federal Government's Response to Environmental Justice (American and Comparative Environmental Policy)*. Cambridge, MA: MIT Press, 2015.

Pauline Maier. *Ratification: The People Debate the Constitution, 1787–1788*. New York, NY: Simon & Schuster, 2011.

Carla Mooney. *The U.S. Constitution: Discover How Democracy Works With 25 Projects*. White River Junction, VT: Nomad Press, 2016.

Ray Raphael. *The U.S. Constitution: Explained—Clause by Clause—for Every American Today.* New York, NY: Vintage Books, 2017.

Periodicals and Internet Sources

Greg Ablavsky, "States battle the federal government for control of public lands. They both have long trampled on Native American rights." Stanford Law School, November 9, 2017. https://law.stanford.edu/2017/11/09/states-battle-the-federal-government-for-control-of-public-lands-they-both-have-long-trampled-on-native-american-rights/

Scott Gaylord, "States Need More Control Over the Federal Government." *New York Times,* July 17, 2013. https://www.nytimes.com/roomfordebate/2013/07/16/state-politics-vs-the-federal-government/states-need-more-control-over-the-federal-government

Jared Meyer and Randal Meyer, "What Many Americans Get Wrong About States' Rights." *Federalist*, July 20, 2015. http://thefederalist.com/2015/07/20/what-many-americans-get-wrong-about-states-rights/

Jeff Nilsson, "The Civil Rights Act vs. States' Rights." *Saturday Evening Post*, July 2, 2014. http://www.saturdayeveningpost.com/2014/07/02/history/post-perspective/the-civil-rights-act-vs-states-rights.html

Michael Tanner, "Marijuana Policy Is Best Left Up to the States." *National Review*, February 28, 2017. http://www.nationalreview.com/article/445289/marijuana-policy-states-rights-issue

"Federal and State Power." *Current Issues: Macmillian Social Science Library*, Macmillan Reference USA, 2003. http://link.galegroup.com/apps/doc/EJ3011400096/OVIC?u=bcps&xid=432d0443

"Federal-State Relations Today: Back to States' Rights?" *US History.org*, 2018. http://www.ushistory.org/gov/3c.asp

"Federal Supremacy vs. States' Rights." North American Law Center, April 23, 2014. http://northamericanlawcenter.org/federal-supremacy-vs-states-rights/#.Wl4_RjdG1PY

"The Question of States' Rights: The Constitution and American Federalism (An Introduction)." *Exploring Constitutional Conflicts*. Accessed January 16, 2018. http://law2.umkc.edu/faculty/projects/ftrials/conlaw/statesrights.html

"Reserved Powers of the States." *The Heritage Guide to the Constitution*, accessed January 16, 2018. https://www.heritage.org/constitution/amendments/10/essays/163/reserved-powers-of-the-states

"The Roles of Federal and State Governments in Education." *Findlaw*, accessed January 16, 2018. http://education.findlaw.com/curriculum-standards-school-funding/the-roles-of-federal-and-state-governments-in-education.html

"State Powers." Constitution USA with Peter Sagal, *PBS*, 2013. http://www.pbs.org/tpt/constitution-usa-peter-sagal/federalism/state-powers/

"States' Rights: Does the federal government exceed its authority?" *Annenberg Classroom*, accessed January 16, 2018. http://www.annenbergclassroom.org/speakout/states-rights

Index

F

G

H